hybnf   HEB
363.7͘ ||| | ||||||||| | | ||| ||||||||||||||| | |||
        ⌇ **W9-AFK-590**

Environmental catastrophe
33410016603484   05/27/20

Hebron Public Library
201 W. Sigler Street
Hebron, IN 46341

Environmental
Catastrophe

Other Books in the Current Controversies Series

Environmental Catastrophe

Bridey Heing, Book Editor

GREENHAVEN
PUBLISHING

Published in 2020 by Greenhaven Publishing, LLC
353 3rd Avenue, Suite 255, New York, NY 10010

Copyright © 2020 by Greenhaven Publishing, LLC

First Edition

All rights reserved. No part of this book may be reproduced in any form
without permission in writing from the publisher, except by a reviewer.

Articles in Greenhaven Publishing anthologies are often edited for length to meet page
requirements. In addition, original titles of these works are changed to clearly present
the main thesis and to explicitly indicate the author's opinion. Every effort is made to
ensure that Greenhaven Publishing accurately reflects the original intent of the authors.
Every effort has been made to trace the owners of the copyrighted material.

Cover image: f00sion/E+/Getty Images

Library of Congress Cataloging-in-Publication Data

Names: Heing, Bridey, editor.
Title: Environmental catastrophe / Bridey Heing, book editor.
Description: First edition. | New York : Greenhaven Publishing, 2020. | Series: Current
controversies | Includes bibliographical references and index. | Audience: Grades 9–12.
Identifiers: LCCN 2019022821 | ISBN 9781534506176 (library
binding) | ISBN 9781534506169 (paperback)
Subjects: LCSH: Environmental disasters—Juvenile literature.
Classification: LCC GE146 .E57 2020 | DDC 363.738/74—dc23
LC record available at https://lccn.loc.gov/2019022821

Manufactured in the United States of America

Website: http://greenhavenpublishing.com

Contents

Chapter 2: Will Environmental Catastrophe Have a Measurable Negative Impact on Daily Life?

Yes: The Impact of Environmental Catastrophe Will Be Significant and Damaging

Severe weather events will worsen and increase in frequency, exacerbating the issues presented by climate change.

Food and Agricultural Organization of the United Nations
Environmental catastrophe will have an impact on food security, leading to shortages and possible starvation in some areas.

No: Steps Are Being Taken to Mitigate the Impacts of Environmental Catastrophe

Lyndsey Gilpin
Innovation in technology is pointing to ways climate change can be addressed, while allowing quality of life to be maintained or improved.

Christopher Cadham
NYC's public-private partnership is an example of how local governments can partner with private stakeholders to mitigate the impact of climate change.

National Climate Change Adaptation Research Facility
Adapting to climate change will be a challenge, but it will reshape our way of life in order to address the impact of environmental catastrophe and climate change in a variety of ways.

Chapter 3: Is Future Environmental Catastrophe Avoidable?

Union of Concerned Scientists
In an ecologically diverse nation like the United States, climate change and environmental catastrophe will have a wide range of effects and manifest in various ways.

Foreword

"Controversy" is a word that has an undeniably unpleasant connotation. It carries a definite negative charge. Controversy can spoil family gatherings, spread a chill around classroom and campus discussion, inflame public discourse, open raw civic wounds, and lead to the ouster of public officials. We often feel that controversy is almost akin to bad manners, a rude and shocking eruption of that which must not be spoken or thought of in polite, tightly guarded society. To avoid controversy, to quell controversy, is often seen as a public good, a victory for etiquette, perhaps even a moral or ethical imperative.

Yet the studious, deliberate avoidance of controversy is also a whitewashing, a denial, a death threat to democracy. It is a false sterilizing and sanitizing and superficial ordering of the messy, ragged, chaotic, at times ugly processes by which a healthy democracy identifies and confronts challenges, engages in passionate debate about appropriate approaches and solutions, and arrives at something like a consensus and a broadly accepted and supported way forward. Controversy is the megaphone, the speaker's corner, the public square through which the citizenry finds and uses its voice. Controversy is the life's blood of our democracy and absolutely essential to the vibrant health of our society.

Our present age is certainly no stranger to controversy. We are consumed by fierce debates about technology, privacy, political correctness, poverty, violence, crime and policing, guns, immigration, civil and human rights, terrorism, militarism, environmental protection, and gender and racial equality. Loudly competing voices are raised every day, shouting opposing opinions, putting forth competing agendas, and summoning starkly different visions of a utopian or dystopian future. Often these voices attempt to shout the others down; there is precious little listening and considering among the cacophonous din. Yet listening and considering, too, are essential to the health of a democracy. If controversy is democracy's lusty lifeblood, respectful listening and careful thought are its higher faculties, its brain, its conscience.

Current Controversies does not shy away from or attempt to hush the loudly competing voices. It seeks to provide readers with as wide and representative as possible a range of articulate voices on any given controversy of the day, separates each one out to allow it to be heard clearly and fairly, and encourages careful listening to each of these well-crafted, thoughtfully expressed opinions, supplied by some of today's leading academics, thinkers, analysts, politicians, policy makers, economists, activists, change agents, and advocates. Only after listening to a wide range of opinions on an issue, evaluating the strengths and weaknesses of each argument, assessing how well the facts and available evidence mesh with the stated opinions and conclusions, and thoughtfully and critically examining one's own beliefs and conscience can the reader begin to arrive at his or her own conclusions and articulate his or her own stance on the spotlighted controversy.

This process is facilitated and supported in each Current Controversies volume by an introduction and chapter overviews that provide readers with the essential context they need to begin engaging with the spotlighted controversies, with the debates surrounding them, and with their own perhaps shifting or nascent opinions on them. Chapters are organized around several key questions that are answered with diverse opinions representing all points on the political spectrum. In its content, organization, and methodology, readers are encouraged to determine the authors' point of view and purpose, interrogate and analyze the various arguments and their rhetoric and structure, evaluate the arguments' strengths and weaknesses, test their claims against available facts and evidence, judge the validity of the reasoning, and bring into clearer, sharper focus the reader's own beliefs and conclusions and how they may differ from or align with those in the collection or those of classmates.

Research has shown that reading comprehension skills improve dramatically when students are provided with compelling, intriguing, and relevant "discussable" texts. The subject matter of these collections could not be more compelling, intriguing, or urgently relevant to today's students and the world they are poised to inherit. The anthologized articles also provide the basis for stimulating, lively, and passionate classroom debates. Students who are compelled to anticipate objections to their own argument and identify the flaws in those of an opponent read more carefully, think more critically, and steep themselves in relevant context, facts, and information more thoroughly. In short, using discussable text of the kind provided by every single volume in the Current Controversies series encourages close reading, facilitates reading comprehension, fosters research, strengthens critical thinking, and greatly enlivens and energizes classroom discussion and participation. The entire learning process is deepened, extended, and strengthened.

If we are to foster a knowledgeable, responsible, active, and engaged citizenry, we must provide readers with the intellectual, interpretive, and critical-thinking tools and experience necessary to make sense of the world around them and of the all-important debates and arguments that inform it. We must encourage them not to run away from or attempt to quell controversy but to embrace it in a responsible, conscientious, and thoughtful way, to sharpen and strengthen their own informed opinions by listening to and critically analyzing those of others. This series encourages respectful engagement with and analysis of current controversies and competing opinions and fosters a resulting increase in the strength and rigor of one's own opinions and stances. As such, it helps readers assume their rightful place in the public square and provides them with the skills necessary to uphold their awesome responsibility—guaranteeing the continued and future health of a vital, vibrant, and free democracy.

Introduction

> *As human beings, we are vulnerable to confusing the unprecedented with the improbable. In our everyday experience, if something has never happened before, we are generally safe in assuming it is not going to happen in the future, but the exceptions can kill you and climate change is one of those exceptions.*
>
> —Al Gore

The science is clear. Our climate is changing and bringing with it shifts in the environment that could imperil the lives of people and animals alike. From rising sea levels to extended periods of drought to unprecedented amounts of rain, climate change is ushering in a time when experts believe that previously rare environmental catastrophes could become commonplace, perhaps even shaping the way we live.

Environmental catastrophes are unique phenomenon specifically caused by mankind. Although an exact definition is difficult to identify, in this book environmental catastrophe refers to changes in environmental conditions that create adverse impacts on human or animal life. This could mean conditions that lead to mass extinctions, loss of agricultural capacity, flooding of coastal areas, or the development of increasingly common severe weather that threatens the quality of life in areas around the world.

Environmental catastrophe can also be caused directly by unintended human action. This includes the 2010 Deepwater

Horizon oil spill, which threatened the biodiversity of the Gulf of Mexico, or the 2011 Fukushima nuclear disaster, which released radioactive material when a tsunami and earthquake resulted in a nuclear meltdown. Environmental catastrophe is generally understood to differ from acts of war, such as the dropping of atomic weapons during World War II, or natural disasters, such as standard avalanches and typhoons that occur regularly throughout the year and are not the result of human activity. This distinction is important; environmental catastrophe is an extreme anomaly that is in many ways unforeseen and has drastic consequences not just in the near future, but potentially for generations.

So what does climate change have to do with environmental catastrophe? Climate change and environmental catastrophe are impossible to separate, as man-made—or anthropogenic—climate change is a driving force in environmental changes that are resulting in dire consequences for the planet. Scientists argue that man-made climate change will lead to environmental catastrophes and in some cases already has. In 2019, the Bramble Cay melomys became the first mammal species to go extinct as a result of man-made climate change when their island habitat was lost to flooding, and in the next fifty years studies indicate that large-scale extinctions could occur. These changes will impact our ability to grow food, the amount of land on which people can reasonably live, the fragile ecosystems that exist around the world, and our public health.

What remains unclear is how we will respond and how much difference it is possible to make. Experts warn that the worst effects of climate change—what amounts to a near constant state of environmental catastrophe that will eventually impact all corners of the globe—can only be headed off in the next decade. A 2018 climate report by the Intergovernmental Panel on Climate Change found that if action is not taken, the temperature of the Earth will rise 3 degrees Celsius above pre-industrial temperatures by 2100; if countries do act, that rise can be limited to 1.5 degrees above pre-industrial temperatures. This lower degree change will still impact our planet in a variety of ways, but not to the severe extent that a rise of 3 degrees would.[1]

There is significant disagreement on all fronts within the climate change and environmental catastrophe debate. Although scientists agree that climate change is man-made and is impacting our planet at an alarming rate, policy makers and members of the public are less united on how to best address the issue. Some are unsure if climate change and environmental catastrophe are linked or if human activity can be fully blamed for the shifts seen in recent decades.

In some cases, that lack of consensus drives the lack of action; some feel climate change and environmental catastrophe must be treated as a threat unlike any other, while others feel we have the time to work out various ways to gradually address the issue. Some feel the best way to do so is with action at a national and international level. The UN, for example, has indicated that a mass mobilization of resources is needed to maintain a lower rise in temperature, and congressional Democrats introduced a Green New Deal in 2019 that would purportedly do so. But others feel this approach would be a threat to the economy and favor instead incremental changes or prioritizing personal choices that address issues of waste and sustainability.

In *Current Controversies: Environmental Catastrophe*, the many questions surrounding climate change and environmental catastrophe are explored in detail. The viewpoints in this book explore the impact climate change currently has and could have around the world, what that impact means for people living in affected areas, and what solutions have been suggested as a means to deal with this issue. Authors look to history and toward the future to examine the question of environmental catastrophe from all angles. While the answer of what will happen to the planet next remains unclear, this collection will give readers the basis on which to form opinions and theories on this critical topic.

Notes

1. "Special Report: Global Warming of 1.5 °C," Intergovernmental Panel on Climate Change (IPCC), https://www.ipcc.ch/sr15/.

CHAPTER 1

Are Nations Doing Enough to Prevent and Recover from Environmental Catastrophes?

A History of Climate Science

Matthew Mason

Matthew Mason is an environmental writer from the UK with a BA in archaeology and MA in landscape archaeology from the University of Exeter.

Humanity has always had an interest in weather patterns. In the last century and a half, wider implications of global temperature and trends and how they might impact the planet, wildlife and humanity have become more studied. Environmental science is the study of the effects of natural and unnatural processes, and of interactions of the physical components of the planet on the environment (particularly human action)[18]. Environmental Science covers a number of disciplines: climatology, oceanography, atmospheric sciences, meteorology, and ecology. It also covers, while having much in common with biology, physics, geology and a lot of other older disciplines. Climate Change is studied under the modern discipline of Environmental Science, which is a branch of Earth Sciences or Atmospheric Sciences and crosses many boundaries, incorporating a wide variety of methods and tools.

19th Century Beginnings

We can trace the history of climate change in environmental science all the way back to the 19th century when there was first proposed the concepts of the "Ice Age" [1] and the "Greenhouse Effect." Even as early as the 1820s, scientists understood the properties of certain gases and their ability to trap solar heat. Though both concepts took a while to finally gain acceptance, once the evidence was beyond dispute—that was when the scientific community began to ask the important questions: how did this happen? What made it happen? Why did the ice age end? Could it happen again? If so,

"History of the Study of Climate Change in Field of Environmental Science," by Matthew Mason, EnvironmentalScience.org. Reprinted by permission.

how soon? The two theories were inextricably linked as researchers first began to propose the idea that lower levels of greenhouse gases in the atmosphere caused ice ages, and that higher levels led to the much warmer temperatures [2].

Even then, understanding the properties of what we today know to be greenhouse gases, scientists in a growing industrialized world first proposed the possibility that the world may eventually face a problem (despite that some proposed industrialization was a positive thing that would prevent the inevitable next ice age— whenever that may be). It was not something to worry about for the immediate future as at the rates the planet was consuming fossil fuels, experts calculated that it would take several thousand years to register significant warming and measurable effects on the climate. As the developed world expanded its industrialization through the 19th century, that figure was adjusted to several centuries [3].

Early 20th Century

The early part of the 20th century saw fierce criticism of the existing theories. Skeptics argued that the concept of global warming was too simplistic and had not taken into account local variations in weather—such as humidity [3]. Flawed tests in the early 19th century were quickly thrown out and for a while most of the scientific field lost interest in the problem [12]. It took until the 1930s for researchers to begin to see the problems that burning fossil fuels was having on the climate. There had been marked changes since the industrial revolution and between the wars, that fact was increasingly noticeable [4]. However, the consensus was that we were entering a phase of natural warming and that the fossil fuels were not having a significant impact on the climate, dissenting voices were treated with skepticism and some (admittedly flawed) tests came back with mixed results [3]. Only Guy Stewart Callendar said that the changes were anthropogenic. In his mind though, it was a positive thing and would merely delay the next ice age [5]. He estimated that the following century would bring a rise of two degrees and recommended researchers take more interest in the data [2].

1940s-1960s

In the 1940s, experts recorded a 1.3C increase in the temperature the North Atlantic since the end of the 19th century [6]; the conclusion was that the only known greenhouse gases then (carbon dioxide and water vapor) were responsible. Studies over the following decade confirmed this temperature rise and it would not be until the 1970s when the other greenhouses gases and their effects would be identified: CFCs, nitrous oxide and methane.

The dawn of the nuclear age in the 1950s and 1960s and the popular imagination's understanding of the damage such weapons could reek upon the planet, gave researchers the opportunity to study the decay of carbon 14 isotopes [3] in the atmosphere. This was, and is, fundamental to our understanding of recent climate change, particularly burning carbon sources. Radiocarbon-14 is used for dating organic objects from recent history—with a limit of up to around 50,000 years [7]. The revelations of Rachel Carson's book *Silent Spring* brought to the public imagination the real effects we may have already had on our planet [8].

The 1950s was also the dawn of the computer era. This was fundamental to the growing interest in the climate. Most importantly, it analyzed each of the layers of the Earth's upper atmosphere [3] far more easily and put to rest the simplistic data and models of the early 20th century. This brought the first confirmation that the increasing levels of carbon dioxide would have a warming effect over time. Furthermore, there was increasing confirmation that doubling of the carbon levels would lead to a global average temperature increase of 3-4 degrees.

Modern Climate Change in Environmental Science: 1970s-1980s

By the time of the 1970s with so much data from a variety of disciplines such as paleontology, paleobotany, archaeology and anthropology led to the understanding that the Earth's climate has always changed and what factors had been forcing it. These new disciplines that brought a wider scope of data sets meant that not only could we see that temperatures were rising, we could see potential consequences too—scientists began speaking of critical changes to the climate from the year 2000. Most tragically on popular opinion, a few fringe writers postulated on the possibility of a new Ice Age to arrive within the next few centuries—but even those experts said the data looked doubtful [3]. The media ran with it and it fuelled for climate skepticism for the next several decades [6].

The international community—both governments and research bodies—were increasingly concerned about what effects our actions would have on the climate and the future of our planet. In 1972, the United Nations formed UNEP—the United Nations Environmental Programme following the first *United Nations Conference on the Human Environment*. They met in Stockholm, Sweden to tackle a range of environmental issues including climate change [9].

Paleodata from ice cores was now fundamental to researching how climate change would affect the global environment and ecosystems and it was during this period that researchers identified massive increase in greenhouse gases from the time of the industrial revolution [6], particularly of methane. The abundance of particles over the 19th century far exceeded all fluctuations of the previous half a million years.

The 1970s was also the era of chlorofluorocarbons (CFCs). They were found to be 10,000 times more effective at absorbing infrared radiation than carbon dioxide. Researchers also quickly discovered the devastating effect the chemical was having on the ozone layer—the layer of gas protecting the Earth from the sun's most harmful rays [13]. Once these damaging properties were confirmed, the substance was banned. This had massive implications for the humble toiletries in our bathrooms as most aerosols contained the chemical. What's more, CFCs were identified as existing purely from industrial operations and did not exist in nature [6].

The evidence was mounting up and 1988 saw the first record hottest year (until that point at least, several more would follow) [2] and the founding of the International Panel on Climate Change (IPCC) [10]. By 1988 we knew that in order to maintain global temperatures, the planet had to radiate as much energy as it received from the sun; we also knew that there was increasingly an imbalance [2]. In the same year, British Prime Minister Margaret Thatcher, whose qualifications were in chemistry, warned of the greenhouse gases being pumped into the atmosphere and warned about the effects they will have in future. She called for a global treaty to tackle the problem for future generations [11].

1990s-Now

The 1990s are considered by many as the "Golden Age" of environmental science. Amongst other things, many of the top climate science journals began in the late 1980s and it was in these years that the discipline truly began to take on board the widest range of data and methods from as broad a scope as possible. It was the dawn of climate modelling on which the IPCC published their reports. The First Assessment Report (FAR) came out in 1990 [6].

Following calls by the UN to act on carbon emissions, protocols set in Montreal and then London sought to phase out these substances most damaging to the environment. In the USA, the Clean Air Act Amendment of 1990 came into force [14] to tackle acid rain, ozone depletion, air pollution and a number of other environmental issues. About the same time, most countries in the western world took steps to introduce similar standards through legislation.

Most critically as far as the science was concerned, ice cores taken from the Antarctic demonstrated that temperature rises preceded the increase in ice levels—this put to rest once and for all the notion that the ice ages were fuelled purely and entirely by the fluctuations in carbon dioxide levels [2]. Ice core data has proven extremely useful in monitoring paleoclimate data. Each layer of snow, each build-up of ice, even each season of ice is different in texture and composition thanks to natural fluctuations. When factoring in larger events, it is relatively straightforward to (when correlated with other data types) work out what the climate was like in any given season [15]. This was crucial in taking study of the climate forward.

Now that the data was becoming more complex, it was time to understand and explain more complex systems, causes and effects. It is a common term now, but in the 1990s the "feedback loop" was a growing hypothesis. Data showed that around the ice ages were massive changes in the environment [6]; each "forcing" (agent) has a different effect on the climate, sometimes positive and sometimes negative, and taking all of these into account required greater levels of modelling and regular fine tuning. Today, the models are considered highly accurate and if anything, the IPCC has underestimated the effects of the various forcing agents on the environment [17]. Climate sensitivity is what it is all about and with millions of years of data to draw conclusions [2]. What they found in the mid 2000s was startling: a doubling of the greenhouse gas levels *always* led to a global temperature increase of 3C in the past.

It is modelling that drives climate study today and though some of the early studies were contradictory, it wasn't until 2005 when researchers began to study the oceans that they could see and understand the full implications of greenhouse gas emissions [2]. Land temperatures rise more rapidly than the oceans which explains why the northern hemisphere has recorded the greater temperature increases, it is distorted by the greater landmass. Overall, we now know that the global mean temperature has already risen 1.53F or 0.8C between 1880 and 2012 [16].

Since the year 2010, there has been a growing occurrence of freak weather incidents. California and Australia have experienced more intense bush fires, Europe has suffered floods and storms, there have been record droughts, record snowfall. November 2013 to February 2014 saw a polar vortex hitting North America, floods and storms in the UK and record warm temperatures in

Siberia. Exceptional wind, record rainfall and a strong jet stream contributed to one of the worst seasons on record.

Sources

1. http://earthobservatory.nasa.gov/Features/Paleoclimatology/paleoclimatology_intro.php

2. http://www.aip.org/history/climate/co2.htm

3. http://www.skepticalscience.com/history-climate-science.html

4. http://www.aip.org/history/climate/summary.htm

5. Bowen, Mark (2006) *Thin Ice*. New York: Henry Holt. p. 96.

6. https://www.ipcc.ch/pdf/assessment-report/ar4/wg1/ar4-wg1-chapter1.pdf

7. https://c14.arch.ox.ac.uk/embed.php?File=dating.html

8. http://orgprints.org/22934/7/22934.pdf

9. http://www.unep.org/about/

10. http://www.ipcc.ch/organization/organization.shtml

11. http://www.margaretthatcher.org/document/107817

12. http://www.aip.org/history/climate/Radmath.htm#L_0141

13. http://www.aip.org/history/climate/othergas.htm

14. http://www.environmentalhistory.org/

15. http://earthobservatory.nasa.gov/Features/Paleoclimatology_IceCores/

16. https://www2.ucar.edu/climate/faq/how-much-has-global-temperature-risen-last-100-years

18. http://www.dailyclimate.org/tdc-newsroom/2012/12/ipcc-climate-predictions

19. http://www.ncl.ac.uk/undergraduate/degrees/f850/courseoverview/

States Are Setting Ambitious Targets to Stall Climate Change

NPR News Staff

National Public Radio (NPR) is a nonprofit news source that provides in-depth reporting on news from around the world.

While nations wrangle over a new global treaty on climate change, the question on many minds is: What happens next?

Key portions of the Kyoto Protocol are set to expire at the end of 2012. But many of the world's major greenhouse gas emitters have already set national targets to reduce emissions, and they're forging their own initiatives to meet those goals.

Some are focusing on curbing deforestation and boosting renewable energy sources. Several nations are experimenting with cap-and-trade plans: Regulators set mandatory limits on industrial emissions, but companies that exceed those "caps" can buy permits to emit from companies that have allowances to spare. In some cases, it's not clear that countries are doing much to meet their stated climate goals. What *is* clear is that the pledges currently on the table aren't legally binding, and they fall far short of what would be required to stabilize the planet's atmosphere.

Here's a look at what nations are doing:

Australia

Australia has set a national goal of reducing greenhouse gas emissions by 5 percent below 2000 levels by 2020.

Australia didn't sign onto the Kyoto Protocol until 2007, after its Labor Party took control of government, reversing the previous administration's policy. Under the climate pact, Australia agreed to hold the growth in its greenhouse gas emissions to 8 percent

©2011 National Public Radio, Inc. NPR news report titled "What Countries Are Doing To Tackle Climate Change" by NPR News Staff was originally published on npr.org on December 9, 2011, and is used with the permission of NPR. Any unauthorized duplication is strictly prohibited.

above 1990 levels for the 2008–2012 period. By and large, Australia has met those targets, mostly by reducing deforestation and land clearing.

In November 2011, Australian lawmakers approved an ambitious carbon trading plan—the world's largest outside of Europe. Under the plan, Australia's 500 worst polluters would be forced to pay a tax on every ton of carbon they emit starting in July 2012. By 2015, the nation plans to move to a full-on, market-based carbon trading system. Australia says it plans to link its carbon market to one set up in neighboring New Zealand. That might make it harder to dismantle the market if conservatives win back control of Australia's government in 2013.

Brazil

Brazil is aiming to reduce its emissions to 1994 levels and cut deforestation by 80 percent *from historic highs by 2020.*

Brazil's National Climate Change Plan is focused on expanding renewable electric energy sources and beefing up the use of biofuels in the transportation industry. The country is also focusing heavily on reducing deforestation rates: It's hoping to eliminate illegal deforestation and bring the net loss of forest coverage to zero by 2015.

But a proposal to loosen Brazil's deforestation rules is currently making its way through the legislature. If enacted, critics say the changes could create more opportunities for logging.

Canada

When Canada signed onto the Kyoto Protocol, it committed to reducing its greenhouse gas emissions by 6 percent below 1990 levels. It later proposed a new, less ambitious goal to reduce emissions by 17 percent from 2005 levels by 2020, a pledge that matches the US.

Canada did little to try to meet its obligations under the Kyoto Protocol. Indeed, today, the country's emissions are 17 percent above 1990 levels—in large part because of emissions tied to the dirty business of extracting oil from Alberta's tar sands.

According to a Canadian government report released in mid-2011, emissions from tar sands will more than cancel out the progress that Canada has made in shifting its electricity generation from coal to natural gas. By 2020, the report projects that Canada will fall well short of its stated emission-reduction targets.

China

China hasn't made any pledges to reduce its carbon emissions. As its economy grows, emissions will increase. But China has promised to become at least 40 percent more energy efficient by 2015.

China is the world's biggest producer and consumer of coal—and the No. 1 emitter of greenhouse gases and the second-largest consumer of energy. But it's also a developing nation—which means that, like other developing nations, it isn't required to lower its emissions under the Kyoto Protocol.

Still, China's coal resources aren't infinite, and as the country finds itself importing more of the fossil fuel to power its growth, it is also aggressively pursuing renewable energy sources. Chinese leaders have said they want non-fossil fuels to account for 15 percent of the nation's energy sources by 2020. Under a law passed in 2005, Chinese power grid companies are required to purchase a certain percentage of their total power supply from renewable energy sources. And China provides extensive subsidies to its clean energy sector—like the US, it hopes that green tech jobs can fuel future growth. Even so, many analysts warn that weaning China off coal won't be easy.

The country has also committed to boosting its forest cover, and it is experimenting with a carbon trading plan: Lawmakers recently approved a pilot program in seven provinces and cities.

European Union

The EU and its 27 member states have pledged to reduce emissions by 20 percent below 1990 levels by 2020. The EU has said it would bump this commitment up to 30 percent if other developed countries sign up for similar commitments.

Under the Kyoto Protocol, the then-15 EU member states signed on to reduce emissions by 8 percent below 1990 levels by 2012. To meet that goal, in 2005 the EU launched the biggest carbon trading market in the world. Today, all 27 member states are required to participate, plus Iceland, Liechtenstein and Norway. Major factories and power plants in the EU are granted permits for how much carbon they can emit. Companies that emit less carbon than their allotted amount can sell their extra carbon credits to firms that exceed their emissions limit.

Starting in January, all airlines with flights that take off or land in Europe will be required to buy carbon permits to offset emissions from their flights. That requirement has sparked objections and legal challenges from several nations that argue it violates international law.

India

India, like China, also won't commit to reducing its carbon emissions—saying that would hurt efforts to bring millions of its citizens out of poverty. But it has agreed to increase its energy efficiency by 20 percent by 2015.

India is the world's No. 3 emitter of greenhouse gases, but because it's a developing nation, it isn't required to cut emissions under the Kyoto Protocol. That said, India is an active participant in the Clean Development Mechanism—a carbon offset plan set up under the Kyoto Protocol. Basically, the CDM lets developing nations like India earn credits for implementing emission-reducing projects. India can then sell those credits to an industrialized nation, which can count them toward its overall emissions-reduction commitment. India has hundreds of CDM projects; almost half of them focus on wind power and biomass.

India has set an ambitious goal of getting 20 gigawatts of solar power online by 2022. A gigawatt of electricity is enough to power a small city. In 2010, the country started levying a carbon tax on coal to help subsidize renewable energy projects.

Indonesia

Indonesia has pledged to cut emissions by 26 percent by 2020 from today's levels.

Indonesia is home to vast swaths of tropical forests, which suck up atmospheric carbon. But those forests are being logged at an alarming rate—and that's releasing huge amounts of carbon into the atmosphere. Under a deal with Norway that went into effect in May 2011, Indonesia agreed to implement a two-year moratorium on new concessions for clearing forests in exchange for $1 billion in support for its forest conservation efforts.

But many observers question Indonesia's commitment to preventing deforestation, given that the country's current economic boom has been largely fueled by extraction of its natural resources. Allegations that Forestry Ministry officials have lined their political war chests with funds raised by selling off logging rights haven't done much to bolster confidence.

Japan

Japan has pledged to reduce its emissions by 25 percent below 1990 levels by 2020.

The world's No. 5 greenhouse gas producer, Japan committed to reducing its emissions by 6 percent below their 1990 levels under the Kyoto Protocol, and it was largely on track to meet that goal. In 2010, it launched a cap-and-trade plan aimed at forcing some 1,300 major businesses—including large office buildings, public buildings and schools—in the Tokyo metropolitan region to reduce their emissions.

However, the Fukushima nuclear disaster threw Japan a fastball. The nation relied on nuclear power for about a third of its electricity, but in the wake of the March 2011 accident, the vast majority of its reactors have gone offline. The lost output forced Japan to institute energy-reducing measures and, in the short term, to rely more heavily on fossil fuel-burning power utilities—which boosted its emissions in 2011. With the Japanese public now wary about nuclear energy, the nation's leaders are trying to find a new way forward.

Russia

Russia has pledged to reduce its emissions by at least 15 percent from 1990 levels—a year when the Soviet Union was still in existence, and emissions from heavy industry, mostly related to the military, were sky high.

When Russia ratified the Kyoto Protocol in 2004, it pledged to hold its greenhouse gas emissions at or below 1990 levels. After the Soviet Union collapsed, Russia's emissions did, too. So the country hasn't had to do much to meet its Kyoto pledges.

Indeed, Russia has long been known as a country with little regard for environmental concerns, and it is still largely dependent on many heavy industries that are considered major polluters. Despite Russian ratification of the climate pact, for a long time the country's leaders continued to question the human role in climate change.

In 2009, the Russian government quietly reversed that position, adopting a new climate doctrine that seemed to accept human contribution to global warming. The same year, the country pledged to reduce its emissions by at least 15 percent from 1990. However, this pledge still doesn't require any action on Russia's part: By some estimates, the country's emissions remain more than 30 percent below 1990 highs. Though Russia has unveiled energy-efficiency goals, analysts call the country's climate policies "a black hole."

South Africa

South Africa expects its emissions to peak between 2020 and 2025, then remain flat for a decade before dropping off. By 2020, South Africa aims for emissions to top out at levels 34 percent lower than if the country were to take no actions.

South Africa is highly dependent on coal—about 90 percent of its electricity comes from burning the fossil fuel—and it's a major contributor to greenhouse gas emissions in Africa. The nation is slowly studying cleaner energy options and more energy-efficient alternatives. But to move forward with any emission reductions, South Africa says it's going to need funding and support from industrialized nations.

South Africa's renewable energy initiative aims to make clean power account for nearly 9 percent of the nation's energy mix by 2030. But that project is just getting off the ground: Construction on the first few dozen projects, mostly wind and solar power plants, won't begin until after mid-2012 at the earliest.

The country says it's committed to making nuclear power—which currently supplies about 5 percent of its electricity—a much bigger part of its energy mix in the future. But a shortage of funding may delay those plans.

United States

The US pledged to reduce emissions by 17 percent by 2020, but that promise was contingent on Congress passing an aggressive cap-and-trade bill. Instead, the bill ended up in the trash, and the US hasn't made it clear how it will meet its emission goals.

The US has taken some actions at the federal level to curb emissions, including new nationwide fuel-efficiency standards for cars and light trucks. Individual states also have laws designed to lower their emissions in the coming decades. California has the most ambitious plan: Starting in 2013, the state will cap greenhouse gas emissions from factories and power plants, and, eventually, emissions from vehicles.

But even with all those state and federal actions taken together, the World Resources Institute figures that the US can't achieve a 17 percent reduction in emissions by 2020. New federal laws—for example, one that puts a tax on carbon emissions—would need to fill the gap, and prospects for that aren't good.

Countries Have Been Working to Mitigate Climate Change for Over Twenty-Five Years

Planete Energies

Planete Energies is an educational website focused on the issue of renewable energy.

C limate change caused by greenhouse gas emissions is, by its very nature, a global issue. A common strategy and binding targets must therefore be defined on a planetary scale. This is the aim of the international climate change conferences held in Rio, Copenhagen and, in December 2015, Paris. The solutions then need to be implemented locally.

Below are some of the key events in the international community's fight against climate change, which began more than 25 years ago.

November 1988 – Creation of the Intergovernmental Panel on Climate Change (IPCC)

Starting in the 1970s, climate science matured, building on advances in numerical modeling and satellite imaging. But to understand and prepare for the challenges of climate change, we needed to share scientific knowledge beyond borders. That's why, at the G7's request, the United Nations set up the Intergovernmental Panel on Climate Change (IPCC) in November 1988. The IPCC's role is to publish reports that provide a clear and up-to-date picture of the current state of scientific knowledge relating to climate change.

June 1992 – Rio Earth Summit

The international community kicked off the fight against climate change in June 1992 in Rio de Janeiro, Brazil, at the second Earth Summit. Following the conference, 166 countries signed the United

"International Efforts to Combat Climate Change," Planete Energies, January 6, 2015. Reprinted by permission.

Nations Framework Convention on Climate Change (UNFCCC), which acknowledges humanity's role in global warming.

Every year, a Conference of the Parties (COP) brings together all of the countries that have ratified the Convention, which now total 195. The next COP will take place in Paris, in December 2015.

December 1997 – Kyoto Protocol

This international emission reduction production sharing contract (or agreement) was adopted on December 11, 1997, at the third Conference of the Parties, in Kyoto, Japan. However, it didn't come into effect until February 2005, because it needed to be ratified by at least 55 countries accounting for at least 55% of the world's emissions. The goal was to reduce emissions of six greenhouse gases by 5.2% between 2008 and 2012, based on 1990 levels. An international carbon market was established to help achieve this goal. The Kyoto Protocol has not been ratified by the United States.

January 2005 – Launch of the European Union Emissions Trading System

In January 2005, the European Union set up its own emissions trading scheme.

Then, in December 2008, the European Union adopted a series of legislative measures, known as the Energy and Climate Package, which sets three targets for 2020: reduce greenhouse emissions by 20%, increase the share of renewable energies in the energy mix to 20% and improve energy efficiency by 20%. This is referred to as the "3 x 20" objective.

December 2009 – Copenhagen Climate Change Conference

The parties to the UNFCCC met in Copenhagen in December 2009 to forge a new agreement to succeed the Kyoto Protocol. Although often considered a failure, the Copenhagen conference can be credited with officially defining the maximum acceptable increase in global temperature as 2°C above pre-industrial levels.

However, the participants were unable to reach a binding agreement on greenhouse gas (ghg) emission reduction targets to keep global warming below this threshold.

The Copenhagen conference was marked by disagreement between developed countries and emerging economies like China, India and Brazil, which believe that measures to reduce greenhouse gas emissions should not impede their economic development. For these countries, the industrialized world is responsible for the damage already done and should therefore provide financial assistance to less-developed economies. For their part, the most industrialized nations have reacted to the economic crisis by shifting their priorities away from incentives and subsidies designed to help combat climate change.

December 2010 – Cancun Climate Change Conference

At the UN Climate Change Conference in Cancun, Mexico, the parties agreed to establish the Green Climate Fund, endowed with $100 billion a year from 2020, to help developing countries combat climate change and deforestation. However, non-governmental organizations have expressed their dissatisfaction with the way in which the fund is financed.

June 2012 – Rio+20 Conference

Twenty years after the Earth Summit that brought climate change to the international community's attention, Rio de Janeiro hosted the fifth United Nations Conference on Sustainable Development, which was attended by government leaders and civil society representatives.

In December 2015, the 21st Conference of the Parties (COP21) to the United Nations Framework Convention on Climate Change (UNFCCC) will be held in Paris, France. The event will be a crucial gathering, since it is tasked with reaching a new international climate agreement, binding on all countries. A COP is held every year, but the 21st session is scheduled to amend the Kyoto

Protocol system, adopted in December 1997 at COP3 and extended essentially unchanged in Doha in 2012 when no agreement could be reached.

The World's Biggest Carbon Dioxide Emitters

According to data published by the International Energy Agency (IEA), global carbon dioxide emissions from fossil fuel combustion totaled 31.3 billion tons in 2011, representing a 2.7% increase from 2010 and a 49.3% increase versus 1990. However, some countries emit more carbon dioxide than others:

- China is the world's biggest carbon dioxide emitter, accounting for 25.5% of global emissions, due its rapid economic growth and extensive reliance on coal. The other top emitters are the United States (16.9%), the 27-member European Union (11.3%), India (5.6%), Russia (5.3%) and Japan (3.8%).
- In Europe, Germany accounts for the most carbon dioxide emissions (748 million tons), followed by the United Kingdom (443 million) and Italy (393 million). France comes in at fourth place, with 328 million tons. The difference is mainly due to power generation systems, since France relies heavily on nuclear power.

The Private Sector Is Responding to Climate Change

Bill Ritter Jr.

Bill Ritter Jr. is the former governor of Colorado and the director of the Center for the New Energy Economy at Colorado State University.

Today, renewable energy resources like wind and solar power are so affordable that they're driving coal production and coal-fired generation out of business. Lower-cost natural gas is helping, too.

I direct Colorado State University's Center for the New Energy Economy, which works with states to facilitate the transition toward a clean energy economy. In my view, today's energy market reflects years of federal and state support for clean energy research, development and deployment.

And, despite the Trump administration's support of coal, a recent survey of industry leaders shows that utilities are not changing their plans significantly.

Transforming Energy Markets

Over the past 24 years—under Presidents Bill Clinton, George W. Bush and Barack Obama—the United States made substantial investments to promote research, development and deployment of clean energy technologies.

Federal agencies provided funding for research and development as well as tax incentives. States used renewable portfolio standards, which typically require that power providers supply an increasing percentage of renewable energy to their customers, to promote deployment of green energy.

"Market Forces Are Driving a Clean Energy Revolution in ihe US," by Bill Ritter, Jr., The Climate Reality Project, July 5, 2018. https://www.climaterealityproject.org/blog/market-forces-are-driving-clean-energy-revolution-us. Licensed under CC BY-ND 3.0.

This one-two punch led to innovations that have transformed US energy markets. In the last eight years, utility-scale solar costs have declined by 86 percent and wind energy prices have fallen by 67 percent.

Natural gas prices, which were highly volatile and often spiked in the early 2000s, have now stabilized at much more affordable levels. They are likely to remain so as production methods improve and sources expand.

The Trump administration is resisting this trend, repealing the Obama administration's Clean Power Plan and proposing subsidies for coal-fired power plants. In doing so, it has also eliminated programs that were designed to help coal-dependent communities weather the energy transition.

But these reversals can do little to change underlying market forces, which are driving innovation, closing coal plants and promoting investment in clean technologies.

Utilities Care About Cost, Predictability and Economic Returns

A recent survey by the trade publication Utility Dive found that electric power industry leaders expect significant growth in solar, wind, natural gas and energy storage. They also project significant decreases in coal- and oil-fired generation.

Why is their outlook so divergent from what's happening in Washington, D.C.? The answer is a result of multiple market dynamics within the energy industry.

- Markets favor low-cost energy. Currently natural gas, wind and solar are the lowest-cost resources available to produce electricity and are pushing out coal as a source of power.
- Markets emphasize the long view. As utilities look at aging coal plants that are providing decreasing value to their systems, they are making multi-decade and multi-billion-dollar decisions on investments in power plants and infrastructure to replace coal.

- Markets loathe uncertainty. The Trump administration's policy reversals and tweets are an unstable foundation upon which to build a corporate strategy.
- Wall Street is helping utilities finance billions of dollars of investment. To ensure access to low-cost capital, they want to cite low-risk investments. Coal represents a high-risk investment from both a pollution and a resource standpoint. In 2016, 44 percent of the US coal supply came from companies that had declared bankruptcy. The resource is simply too risky for investment markets.
- Utilities earn returns on investments in capital infrastructure. Investments in renewable resources are nearly all capital investment and represent the best return for investors.

Integration and Technology Advances Support Renewables

There are, of course, renewable energy skeptics. Detractors argue that wind and sun are intermittent sources—not reliable 24 hours a day as a resource that can be turned on and off in response to power market demands.

This is partially true: A single solar field only produces energy when the sun is shining, and a single wind farm only produces energy while the wind is blowing.

But as these resources expand geographically, they create an integrated system of renewable generation that produces a consistent source of electricity.

States in New England, mid-Atlantic and the Midwest have integrated electricity systems run by independent system operators that deliver power over large geographic areas, enabling them to balance energy output across their territories.

Now the West, too, is starting to integrate into regional transmission systems powered largely by clean sources.

For example, in Colorado, Xcel Energy recently submitted a plan to regulators to replace coal generation with renewables and natural gas. This shift will bring its Colorado mix of power up to

55 percent renewable by 2026 while reducing associated emissions 60 percent below 2005 levels—all without the EPA's Clean Power Plan or a renewable mandate. Xcel is also finalizing plans to join the Southwest Power Pool, a transmission market that includes nine other states.

Further, advances in energy storage are decreasing the intermittency of renewable generation and offering utilities a buffer between energy demand and energy supply.

With storage, utilities can deliver energy when the system needs it. They also can meet spikes in demand with energy from batteries, which reduces the need to build expensive generation that is needed only to meet peak power demand.

Innovation is also giving utilities and consumers new ways to manage their power needs. More energy-efficient buildings and appliances, and the ability to manage power requirements through an intelligent grid, will make it possible to do more with less electricity, lowering energy costs for everyone.

I expect this dramatic transition to become more pronounced over the next 15 to 20 years. US energy production and consumption will continue to evolve toward a cleaner, more stable and more intelligent system.

This is good news for US energy consumers and for efforts to protect our climate, environment and economy for future generations.

So Far, Countries Have Not Done Enough to Meaningfully Address Climate Change

Fiona Harvey

Fiona Harvey is an award-winning environmental journalist who writes for the Guardian.

Countries are failing to take the action needed to stave off the worst effects of climate change, a UN report has found, and the commitments made in the 2015 Paris agreement will not be met unless governments introduce additional measures as a matter of urgency.

New taxes on fossil fuels, investment in clean technology and much stronger government policies to bring down emissions are likely to be necessary. Governments must also stop subsidising fossil fuels, directly and indirectly, the UN said.

Gunnar Luderer, one of the authors of the UN report and senior scientist at the Potsdam Institute for Climate Impact Research in Germany, said: "There is still a tremendous gap between words and deeds, between the targets agreed by governments and the measures to achieve these goals.

"Only a rapid turnaround here can help. Emissions must be reduced by a quarter by 2030 [to keep warming to no more than 2C (3.6F) above pre-industrial levels] and for 1.5C emissions would have to be halved."

In all, a tripling of effort may be needed to keep warming to less than 2C, meeting scientific advice on avoiding the most dangerous effects of climate change.

Greenhouse gas emissions continued their long-term rise last year, according to the UN, but they could be brought under control. There are promising signs, such as investment from the private

"World Must Triple Efforts or Face Catastrophic Climate Change, Says UN," by Fiona Harvey, Guardian News and Media Limited, November 27, 2018. Reprinted by permission.

sector in renewable energy and other technologies to cut carbon, but these are currently insufficient to meet scientific advice.

Joyce Msuya, deputy executive director of UN Environment, said: "The science is clear: for all the ambitious climate action we've seen, governments need to move faster and with greater urgency. We're feeding this fire, while the means to extinguish it are within reach."

Global emissions have reached what the UN has called "historic levels" of 53.5 gigatonnes of carbon dioxide equivalent, and are showing no signs of peaking, despite a levelling off in the past decade.

The report came a day after Donald Trump said he did not believe his own administration's latest report warning about the dire risk of inaction on climate change.

Last month, the Intergovernmental Panel on Climate Change warned of the dire effects of allowing global warming to reach 1.5C above pre-industrial levels. The world has a little over a decade to bring down greenhouse gas emissions before such dangerous levels of warming become inevitable.

Only 57 countries, representing 60% of global greenhouse gas emissions, are on track to cause their emissions to peak before 2030. If emissions are allowed to rise beyond that, the IPCC has said countries are likely to breach the 1.5C limit, which will trigger sea-level rises, droughts, floods and other extreme weather events.

On Monday, the biggest review of climate change in the UK for a decade found that flooding was likely to become more severe and summers could become more than 5C hotter within 50 years.

The UN's warning comes before key talks in Poland next month, when governments will meet to discuss how to implement the commitments made in Paris in 2015. According to the Paris agreement, the first global pact to bind both developed and developing countries to a specific temperature goal, governments must do all they can to stop warming reaching 2C above pre-industrial levels, with an aspiration to limit warming to no more than 1.5C.

Jian Liu, the chief scientist at UN Environment, said some of the necessary policies were clear and available, if there was political will to implement them. "When governments embrace fiscal policy measures to subsidise low-carbon alternatives and tax fossil fuels, they can stimulate the right investments in the energy sector and significantly reduce carbon emissions. If all fossil fuel subsidies were phased out, global carbon emissions could be reduced by up to 10% by 2030."

Carbon pricing is one way of achieving this, but has run into difficulties as taxes are often unpopular and schemes to reduce carbon through emissions trading are often contested by businesses and other interests.

Greenhouse gas emissions stalled soon after the global financial crisis of a decade ago, then quickly resumed their rise, to the consternation of climate experts. For three years before 2017 they fell once again, but last year there was an increase. Emissions are expected to rise further this year, pointing to an emissions gap between what countries promised in Paris and what their policies are delivering.

Another problem is that infrastructure such as buildings, transport networks and energy generation that is built now to rely on fossil fuels will in effect lock in future emissions for the lifetime in which that infrastructure operates, usually up to 50 years.

Changing the way we construct infrastructure is therefore essential, but many companies and governments still rely on old measures of economic performance and old ways of generating energy and constructing buildings.

Jennifer Morgan, the executive director of Greenpeace International, said: "The window of opportunity is starting to close and if we fail to act now the opportunity will be gone. Failure to act will lock in catastrophic global warming that will change the planet irrevocably and condemn millions to suffering. What are governments waiting for?"

Stephanie Pfeifer, the chief executive of the Institutional Investors Group on Climate Change, said some businesses were taking action. "Investors understand the opportunity presented by the move to a low-carbon economy. The right signals from government will help to unlock low-carbon investment from the private sector."

The States Most Responsible for Climate Change Are Not Doing Enough to Help Those Vulnerable to Its Effects

Glenn Althor, James E. M. Watson, and Richard A. Fuller

Glenn Althor is a research assistant at FoodLab Sydney. James E. M. Watson heads the Wildlife Conservation Society's climate change program and is an adjunct associate professor at the University of Queensland in Australia. Richard A. Fuller leads the Fuller Lab at the School of Biological Sciences, University of Queensland.

The current generation is the first to feel the effects of anthropogenic climate change. Despite their well-known harmful impacts to the world's climate system, greenhouse gases (GHG) are deliberately emitted by countries to drive economic growth and enhance human wellbeing. Spatially localised environmental issues, such as city air pollution, may result from high GHG emissions, but the most damaging and long lasting consequence, that of global climate change, is not constrained within the border of the emitting country. Rather, by polluting the Earth's atmosphere with GHG emissions through fossil fuel combustion, deforestation and agricultural activities, emitting countries are degrading the world's climate system, a common resource shared by all biodiversity, including people.

Because the impacts of GHG emissions can be felt beyond a country's border, and the impacts of climate change on countries are highly variable, there is potential for some emitters to contribute more or less to the causes of climate change than is proportionate to their vulnerability to its effects. This inequity has not gone

"Global Mismatch Between Greenhouse Gas Emissions and the Burden of Climate Change," by Glenn Althor, James E. M. Watson, and Richard A. Fuller, Scientific Reports, February 5, 2016, https://www.nature.com/articles/srep20281. Licensed under CC BY 4.0 International

unnoticed in international climate negotiations or global reporting. As far back as 1992, the United Nations Framework Convention on Climate Change (UNFCCC) committed to the principle of "common but differentiated responsibilities", in which countries have a common responsibility in reducing GHG emissions, but historic emissions and differences in current development levels mean that countries have different levels of emissions reduction obligations. Both of the previous IPCC Assessment Reports have acknowledged the inequity in the causes and effects of climate change although operationalising the principle has proved difficult This is primarily because developing and developed countries continue to disagree over the extent of each other's responsibilities. One major impediment to resolving such debates is a poor quantitative understanding of the magnitude of the global inequity in emissions and impacts. 'Free rider' countries contribute disproportionately to global GHG emissions with only limited vulnerability to the effects of the resulting climate change, while 'forced rider' countries are most vulnerable to climate change but have contributed little to its genesis. This is an issue of environmental equity on a truly global scale.

Here, we measure the current pattern of global climate change equity, and assess whether the situation will improve or worsen by 2030, using data on GHG emissions and newly available national climate change vulnerability assessments. We address the lack of a contemporary, qualitative assessment of global climate equity that incorporates key variables. Previous studies have been limited to CO_2 emissions datasets, omitting the most potent and long lasting GHGs, and used vulnerability variables that do not capture the complexity of climate change threats, and cannot be forecasted. Here, we use the most recently available datasets based on comprehensive national vulnerability assessments and comprehensive GHG emissions data to produce an easily replicable snapshot of the relationship between countries' GHG emissions and their vulnerability to the negative effects of climate change, and forecast this to 2030. We employ economic metrics, the Gini and

Robin Hood coefficients, to quantify the present level of equity in GHG emissions. Only through a proper empirical understanding of the pattern of climate equity now, and how it will change in the near future, can signatories of the UNFCCC make meaningful progress toward resolving the inequity in the burden of climate change impacts.

Results

Greenhouse gas emissions are spread highly unevenly across the world's countries, with the top ten GHG emitting countries generating >60% of total emissions, and three countries, China (21.1%), the United States of America (14.1%) and India (5.2%) being by far the largest contributors. A Gini coefficient of 80.9 indicated extreme inequality in the distribution of emissions among countries, given that the index can only vary between 0 (perfectly even responsibility) and 100 (one country responsible for all emissions). A Robin Hood index of 64 indicated that 64% of GHG emissions would need to be redistributed to achieve an even distribution among countries. Vulnerability to the impacts of climate change was also unevenly spread among countries, with 17 countries acutely vulnerable to climate change impacts in 2010. The majority of these were island countries located in the Atlantic, Pacific and Indian oceans and African countries. By 2030 the number of acutely vulnerable countries is predicted to rise dramatically, and the majority of these will again be island and African countries.

Countries least vulnerable to the impacts of climate change were generally the highest GHG emitters, and conversely those most vulnerable to climate change were the least responsible for its genesis. This inequity held true for both 2010 and 2030, with a negative relationship between emissions and climate vulnerability in both years. The only exception is in 2030, where countries acutely vulnerable to climate change will have slightly higher average emissions than those in the severe category.

In 2010, of the 179 countries assessed, 28 (15.6%) were in the same quintile for GHG emissions and vulnerability to the negative impacts of climate change. This indicates that their vulnerability to climate change approximately matched their relative contribution to its genesis. Ninety countries (50.3%) had GHG emissions in a higher quintile than their 2010 climate vulnerability, and 20 (11.2%) countries were free riders, with GHG emissions in the highest quintile and climate vulnerability in the lowest quintile. Sixty-one (34%) countries had GHG emissions in a lower quintile than their climate vulnerability, and six (3.4%) countries were forced riders, with GHG emissions in the lowest quintile and climate vulnerability in the highest quintile (Comoros, Gambia, Guinea-Bissau, São Tomé and Príncipe, Solomon Islands and Vanuatu).

By 2030, climate change inequity will rise further, with an increase in the proportion of countries that are forced riders, but fewer free riders and equitable countries. Free riders are typically located in the world's sub-tropical and temperate regions, while forced riders are frequently located in tropical regions.

Greenhouse gas emissions were positively correlated with GDP, while climate vulnerability declined with increasing GDP. Our analysis considers the absolute contribution of each country to climate change, but we also examined climate change equity in per capita terms to provide a more complete picture of emissions responsibilities. The patterns were broadly similar, with, for example, Australia, Russia and the United States of America remaining free riders. However, several populous major emitters (e.g. United Kingdom, China, and Brazil) were no longer categorised as free riders.

Discussion

Climate change inequity is globally pervasive, and correlated with economic output. Some countries, such as China and the United States of America, are in a win-win position of achieving economic growth through fossil fuel use with few consequences from the resulting climate change, while many other, mostly Island

and African, countries suffer low economic growth and severe, negative climate change impacts. The beneficiaries of this climate inequity have few incentives to meaningfully reduce or halt their GHG emissions. Despite many of the broad issues around climate equity being well known, well-funded global mechanisms that are being implemented still do not exist. This has serious consequences for our ability to slow the rate of climate change, and reduce the wellbeing implications for forced rider countries.

There are several global policy frameworks currently being debated that could address elements of the problem. The Paris Agreement, secured at the 21st UNFCCC Conference of the Parties (COP21), for example, sets an ambitious target of limiting global warming to 1.5°C above preindustrial levels. However, the 160 indicative nationally determined contributions (INDCs) pledges submitted by signatories to the UNFCCC prior to COP21, indicate that current targets for GHG emissions are unlikely to limit warming to below 2°C With no binding agreement established at COP21 for INDCs, there is no clear indication of how successful the Paris Agreement will be. Addressing GHG emissions is clearly an important first step in ensuring the burden of climate change is not amplified in the future. However, the historic commitment to GHG emissions reduction by key free riders has been slow. Only 50 countries ratified the previous Doha Amendment to the Kyoto protocol, which did not include key free riders such as the United States and Russia. Furthermore, some countries have actually backtracked on their commitments to emissions reductions (e.g. Canada and Australia).

Likewise, the Paris Agreement calls for urgent and adequate financing of US$100 billion per year by 2020 for climate mitigation and adaptation through the Financial Mechanism of the Convention (FMC). However, there is no legally binding mechanism under which parties are responsible for providing this funding. History suggests such funding goals are not always met. For example, the Green Climate Fund (GCF) was established in 2010 under the UNFCCC to mobilise funding support for the least developed countries that are most vulnerable to climate change, yet it remains poorly funded, with only US$10.2 billion received in pledges by November 2015. Addressing these issues around climate funding will play a critical role in addressing climate inequity

Conclusion

It is clear climate change inequity must be addressed. If the commitment to the principle of common but differentiated responsibilities that was widely accepted early on in the UNFCCC is to be acted upon, member states now need to do much more to hold climate free riders to account. To ensure equitable outcomes from climate negotiations, there needs to be a meaningful mobilization of policies, such as the Paris Agreement, that achieve national level emissions reductions, and to ensure the vulnerable forced-rider countries are able to adapt rapidly to climate change. The provisioning of these policy mechanisms will require a distribution of resources and responsibilities and we believe our results provide one way to understand where these responsibilities lie. The Paris Agreement may be a significant step forward in global climate negotiations. However, as the Agreement's key policies are yet to be realized, member states have both an exceptional opportunity and a moral impetus to use these results to address climate change equity in a meaningful manner.

Countries Working Alone Cannot Address Climate Change

BC Campus

BC Campus is an open-source educational platform based in British Columbia, Canada.

M any countries around the world have become more aware of the benefits of environmental protection. Yet even if most nations individually took steps to address their environmental issues, no nation acting alone can solve certain environmental problems which spill over national borders. No nation by itself can reduce emissions of carbon dioxide and other gases by enough to solve the problem of global warming—not without the cooperation of other nations. Another issue is the challenge of preserving biodiversity, which includes the full spectrum of animal and plant genetic material. Although a nation can protect biodiversity within its own borders, no nation acting alone can protect biodiversity around the world. Global warming and biodiversity are examples of international externalities.

Bringing the nations of the world together to address environmental issues requires a difficult set of negotiations between countries with different income levels and different sets of priorities. If nations such as China, India, Brazil, Mexico, and others are developing their economies by burning vast amounts of fossil fuels or by stripping their forest and wildlife habitats, then the world's high-income countries acting alone will not be able to reduce greenhouse gases. However, low-income countries, with some understandable exasperation, point out that high-income countries do not have much moral standing to lecture them on the necessities of putting environmental protection ahead of economic

"International Environmental Issues," BC Campus Open Education. https://opentextbc.ca/principlesofeconomics/chapter/12-5-international-environmental-issues/. Licensed under CC BY 4.0 International.

growth. After all, high-income countries have historically been the primary contributors to greenhouse warming by burning fossil fuels—and still are today. It is hard to tell people who are living in a low-income country, where adequate diet, health care, and education are lacking, that they should sacrifice an improved quality of life for a cleaner environment.

Can rich and poor countries come together to address global environmental spillovers? At the initiative of the European Union and the most vulnerable developing nations, the Durban climate conference in December 2011 launched negotiations to develop a new international climate change agreement that covers all countries. The agreement will take the form of an agreed upon outcome with legal force applicable to all parties. According to the EU, the goal is to adopt the plan in 2015 and implement it in 2020. For the agreement to work, the two biggest emitters of greenhouse gases—China and the United States—will have to sign on.

If high-income countries want low-income countries to reduce their emissions of greenhouse gases, then the high-income countries may need to pay some of the costs. Perhaps some of these payments will happen through private markets; for example, some tourists from rich countries will pay handsomely to vacation near the natural treasures of low-income countries. Perhaps some of the transfer of resources can happen through making modern pollution-control technology available to poorer countries.

The practical details of what such an international system might look like and how it would operate across international borders are forbiddingly complex. But it seems highly unlikely that some form of world government will impose a detailed system of environmental command-and-control regulation around the world. As a result, a decentralized and market-oriented approach may be the only practical way to address international issues such as global warming and biodiversity.

Key Concepts and Summary

Certain global environmental issues, such as global warming and biodiversity, spill over national borders and will need to be addressed with some form of international agreement.

CHAPTER 2

Will Environmental Catastrophe Have a Measurable Negative Impact on Daily Life?

Environmental Catastrophe Impacts Countries in Various Ways

United States Environmental Protection Agency

The Environmental Protection Agency (EPA) is a federal agency that oversees environment-related policies in the United States.

Human basic needs, such as food, water, health, and shelter, are affected by climate. Changes in climate may threaten these needs with increased temperatures, sea level rise, changes in precipitation, and more frequent or intense extreme events.

Climate change will affect individuals and groups differently. Certain groups of people are particularly sensitive to climate change impacts, such as the elderly, the infirm, children and pregnant women, native and tribal groups, and low-income populations.

Climate change may also threaten key natural resources, affecting water and food security. Conflicts, mass migrations, health impacts, or environmental stresses in other parts of the world could raise economic, health, and national security issues for the United States.

Although climate change is an inherently global issue, the impacts will not be felt equally across the planet. Impacts are likely to differ in both magnitude and rate of change in different continents, countries, and regions. Some nations will likely experience more adverse effects than others. Other nations may benefit from climate changes. The capacity to adapt to climate change can influence how climate change affects individuals, communities, countries, and the global population.

"International Climate Impacts," United States Environmental Protection Agency, December 20, 2016.

Impacts on Basic Needs

Impacts on Agriculture and Food

Changes in climate could have significant impacts on food production around the world. Heat stress, droughts, and flooding events may lead to reductions in crop yields and livestock productivity. Areas that are already affected by drought, such as Australia and the Sahel in Africa, will likely experience reductions in water available for irrigation.

At middle to high latitudes, cereal crop yields are projected to increase slightly, depending on local rates of warming and crop type. At lower latitudes, cereal crop yields are projected to decrease. The greatest decreases in crop yields will likely occur in dry and tropical regions. In some African countries, for example, wheat yields could decline by as much as 35% by 2050.

Climate change is affecting many fisheries around the world. Increasing ocean temperatures have shifted some marine species to cooler waters outside of their normal range. Fisheries are important for the food supply and economy of many countries. For example, more than 40 million people rely on the fish caught in the Lower Mekong delta in Asia, which is the largest freshwater fishery in the world. Projected reductions in water flows and increases in sea level may negatively affect water quality and fish species in regions like these, affecting the food supply for communities that depend on these resources.

Climate change is very likely to affect global, regional, and local food security by disrupting food availability, decreasing access to food, and making utilization more difficult. Climate risks to food security are greatest for poor populations and in tropical regions. The potential of climate change to affect global food security is important for food producers and consumers in the United States.

Impacts on Water Supply and Quality

Semi-arid and arid areas (such as the Mediterranean, southern Africa, and northeastern Brazil) are particularly vulnerable to the impacts of climate change on water supply. Over the next century, these areas will likely experience decreases in water resources, especially in areas that are already water-stressed due to droughts, population pressures, and water resource extraction.

As climate changes, water is very likely to become scarce at least part of the time in many areas, but more plentiful part of the time in some areas as well. The availability of water is strongly related to the amount and timing of runoff and precipitation. With a 2.7°F rise in global mean temperature, annual average streamflow is projected to increase by 10-50% at high latitudes and in some wet tropical areas, but decrease by 10-50% in some dry regions at mid-latitudes and in the subtropics. As temperatures rise, snowpack is declining in many regions and glaciers are melting at unprecedented rates, making water less available in areas that depend on it from melting snow and glaciers during spring and summer. Droughts are likely to become more widespread. When it does rain, more precipitation is expected to fall in extreme heavy precipitation events. Increases in heavy precipitation events would not increase water supply, but instead result in increased flooding, except in river basins with large dams able to hold excess water until it is needed.

Water quality is important for ecosystems, human health and sanitation, agriculture, and other purposes. Increases in temperature, changes in precipitation, sea level rise, and extreme events could diminish water quality in many regions. Large rainstorms may cause large amounts of pollutants to enter rivers and estuaries, as excess water may overwhelm wastewater systems and natural buffers. Increased pollution as well as increasing water temperatures can cause algal blooms and potentially increase bacteria in water bodies. In coastal areas and small islands, saltwater from rising sea level and storm surges threaten water supplies. These impacts may require communities to begin treating their water in order to provide safe water resources for human uses.

Impacts on Human Health

The risks of climate-sensitive diseases and health impacts can be high in countries that have little capacity to prevent and treat illness. There are many examples of health impacts related to climate change.

- Increases in temperatures are linked to more frequent and severe heat stress.
- Worsened air quality that often accompanies heat waves or wildfires can lead to breathing problems and exacerbate respiratory and cardiovascular diseases.
- Impacts of climate change on agriculture and other food systems can increase rates of malnutrition and foodborne illnesses.
- Climate changes can influence infectious diseases. The spread of meningococcal (epidemic) meningitis is often linked to climate changes, especially drought. Areas of sub-Saharan and West Africa are sensitive to the spread of meningitis, and will be particularly at-risk if droughts become more frequent and severe.
- The spread of mosquito-borne diseases such as malaria, dengue, and West Nile virus may increase in areas projected to receive more precipitation and flooding. Increases in rainfall and temperature can cause spreading of dengue fever.
- Changes in precipitation patters and extreme weather events can lead to cascading health impacts, particularly when power, water, or transportation systems are disrupted. Diarrheal diseases from contaminated water and food sources are a major concern, particularly for children.
- The effects of global climate change on mental health and well-being are integral parts of the overall climate-related human health impacts. Mental health consequences of climate change range from minimal stress and distress symptoms to clinical disorders, such as anxiety, depression, post-traumatic stress, and suicidal thoughts.

Certain groups of people in low-income countries are especially at risk for adverse health effects from climate change. These at-risk groups include urban people living in poverty, older adults, young children, traditional societies, subsistence farmers, and coastal populations. Many regions, such as Europe, South Asia, Australia, and North America, have experienced heat-related health impacts. Rural populations, older adults, outdoor workers, and those without access to air conditioning are often the most vulnerable to heat-related illness and death.

Impacts on Shelter

Climate change affects the migration of people within and between countries around the world. A variety of reasons may force people to migrate into other areas. These reasons include conflicts, such as ethnic or resource conflicts, degraded ecosystem services, such as lack of viable agricultural land or fresh water, and extreme events, such as flooding, drought, and hurricanes. Extreme events displace many people, especially in areas that do not have the ability or resources to quickly respond or rebuild after disasters. Many types of extreme events are becoming more frequent or severe because of climate change, which exacerbates existing conflicts. This will likely increase the numbers of people migrating during and after these types of events.

Coastal settlements and low-lying areas are particularly vulnerable to climate change impacts, such as sea level rise, erosion, and extreme storms. Rising ocean temperatures and acidity may also threaten coastal ecosystems. As coastal habitats (such as barrier islands, wetlands, deltas, and estuaries) are destroyed, coastal settlements can become more vulnerable to flooding from storm surges and erosion. Both developing and developed countries are vulnerable to the impacts of sea level rise. For example, Bangladesh, the Netherlands, and Guyana are particularly at-risk.

[…]

Regional Impacts

Highlights of recent and projected regional impacts are shown below.

Impacts on Africa

- Africa may be the most vulnerable continent to climate variability and change because of multiple existing stresses and low adaptive capacity. Existing stresses include poverty, food insecurity, political conflicts, and ecosystem degradation.
- By 2050, between 350 million and 600 million people are projected to experience increased water stress due to climate change. Urban population is also projected to triple, increasing by 800 million people, complicating urban poverty and access to basic services.
- Climate variability and change is projected to severely compromise agricultural production, including access to food, in many African countries and regions.
- Toward the end of the 21st century, projected sea level rise will likely affect low-lying coastal areas with large populations, including Senegal, Liberia, and Mozambique.
- Climate variability and change can negatively impact human health. In many African countries, existing health threats—such as malnutrition, malaria and other vector-borne diseases—can be exacerbated by climate change.

Impacts on Asia

- Glaciers in Asia are retreating at faster rates than ever documented in historical records. Some glaciers currently cover 20% of the land that they covered a century ago. Melting glaciers increase the risks of flooding and rock avalanches from destabilized slopes.
- Climate change is projected to decrease freshwater availability, especially in central and southeast Asia, particularly in large river basins. With population growth and increasing demand

from higher standards of living, this decrease could adversely affect more than a billion people by 2050.

- Increased flooding from the sea and, in some cases, from rivers threatens coastal areas, especially heavily populated delta regions in south and southeast Asia.
- The impacts of climate change on crop yields are likely to vary drastically depending on region, crop type, and regional changes in temperature and precipitation. For example, by the mid-21st century, climate change could increase crop yield up to 20% in east and southeast Asia, while decreasing yield up to 30% in central and south Asia.
- Sickness and death due to diarrheal disease will likely increase in east, south, and southeast Asia due to projected changes in the hydrological cycle associated with climate change.

Impacts on Australia and New Zealand

- Water security problems are projected to intensify with a 1°C global average warming in southwestern and southeastern Australia, and in the northern and some eastern parts of New Zealand.
- Biodiversity within some ecologically rich sites, including the Great Barrier Reef and Queensland Wet Tropics, will be at significant risk by 2050.
- Sea level rise and more severe storms and coastal flooding will continue to affect coastal areas. Coastal development and population growth in areas such as Cairns and Southeast Queensland (Australia) and Northland to Bay of Plenty (New Zealand), would place more people and infrastructure at risk.
- Increased drought and fire are projected to cause declines in agricultural and forestry production over much of southern Australia and the northern and eastern parts of New Zealand.
- Cascading and interacting economic, social, and daily life circumstances have accompanied prolonged drought in rural regions. Drought-related worry and psychological distress increased in drought-declared Australian regions,

particularly for those experiencing loss of livelihood and industry. Long-term drought has been linked to increased incidence of suicide among male farmers in Australia.

- Extreme storm events are likely to increase the failure of dikes, levees, drainage, and sewerage systems. They are also likely to increase the damage from storms and fires.
- More heat waves are likely to cause more deaths and more electrical blackouts.
- Indigenous populations are more exposed the risks of climate change than most other Australians and New Zealanders.

Impacts on Europe

- Wide-ranging impacts of climate change are already being documented in Europe, including retreating glaciers, sea level rise, longer growing seasons, species range shifts, and heat wave-related health impacts.
- Future impacts of climate change will likely negatively affect nearly all European regions, with adverse social, health, and infrastructure effects. Many economic sectors, such as agriculture and energy, could face challenges.
- In southern Europe, higher temperatures and drought may reduce water availability, hydropower potential, summer tourism, and crop productivity, hampering economic activity more than other European regions.
- In central and eastern Europe, summer precipitation is projected to decrease, causing higher water stress. Forest productivity is projected to decline. The frequency of peatland fires is projected to increase.
- In northern Europe, climate change is initially projected to bring mixed effects, including some benefits such as reduced demand for heating, increased crop yields, and increased forest growth. However, as climate change continues, negative impacts are likely to outweigh benefits. These include more frequent winter floods, endangered ecosystems, and increasing ground instability from thawing permafrost.

Impacts on Central and South America

- By mid-century, increases in temperature and decreases in soil moisture are projected to cause savanna to gradually replace tropical forest in eastern Amazonia.
- In drier areas, climate change will likely worsen drought, leading to salinization (increased salt content) and desertification (land degradation) of agricultural land. The productivity of livestock and some important crops such as maize and coffee is projected to decrease in some areas, with adverse consequences for food security. In temperate zones, soybean yields are projected to increase.
- Sea level rise is projected to increase risk of flooding, displacement of people, salinization of drinking water resources, and coastal erosion in low-lying areas. These risks threaten fish stocks, recreation, and tourism.
- Changes in precipitation patterns and the melting of glaciers are projected to significantly affect water availability for human consumption, agriculture, and energy generation.
- Climate change and land use changes are expected to increase the rates of species extinction.
- Warmer weather, milder winters, and changes in precipitation may increase incidence of some vector-borne diseases, such as the chikungunya virus, which is transmitted by mosquitoes.

Impacts on North America

- Warming in western mountains will decrease snowpack, increase winter flooding, and reduce summer flows, exacerbating competition for over-allocated water resources.
- Disturbances from pests, diseases, and fire are projected to increasingly affect forests, with extended periods of high fire risk and large increases in area burned.
- Moderate climate change in the early decades of the century is projected to increase aggregate yields of rain-fed agriculture in northern areas, but temperature increases will reduce

corn, soy, and cotton yields in the Midwest and South by 2020. Crops that are near the warm end of their suitable range or that depend on highly utilized water resources will likely face major challenges. High emissions scenarios project reductions in yields by as much as 80% by the end of the century.

- Increases in the number, intensity, and duration of heat waves during the course of the century are projected to further challenge cities that currently experience heat waves, with potential for adverse health impacts and increased stress on energy systems. Older populations are most at risk.

- Climate change will likely increasingly stress coastal communities and habitats, worsening the existing stresses of population, development, and pollution on infrastructure, human health, and the ecosystem.

Impacts on Polar Regions

- Climate changes will likely reduce the thickness and extent of glaciers and ice sheets.

- Changes in natural ecosystems will likely have detrimental effects on many organisms including migratory birds, mammals, and higher predators as marine species shift their ranges.

- In the Arctic, climate changes will likely reduce the extent of sea ice and permafrost, which can have mixed effects on human settlements. Negative impacts could include damage to infrastructure and changes to winter activities such as ice fishing and ice road transportation. Positive impacts could include more navigable northern sea routes.

- The reduction and thawing of permafrost, sea level rise, and stronger storms may worsen coastal erosion and disrupt both natural and social systems.

- Climate change effects—such as increases in coastal erosion, changes in the ranges of some fish, increased weather unpredictability—are already disrupting traditional hunting and subsistence practices of indigenous Arctic communities, and may force relocation of villages.

- Terrestrial and marine ecosystems and habitats are projected to be at risk to invasive species, as climatic barriers are lowered in both polar regions.

Impacts on Small Islands

- Small islands, whether located in the tropics or higher latitudes, are highly vulnerable to extreme weather events, changes in sea level, increases in air and surface temperatures, and changing rainfall patterns.
- Deterioration in coastal conditions, such as beach erosion and coral bleaching, will likely affect local resources such as fisheries, as well as the value of tourism destinations.
- Sea level rise is projected to worsen inundation, storm surge, erosion, and other coastal hazards. These impacts would threaten vital infrastructure, settlements, and facilities that support the livelihood of island communities.
- By mid-century, on many small islands (such as the Caribbean and Pacific), climate change is projected to reduce already limited water resources to the point that they become insufficient to meet demand during low-rainfall periods.
- Invasion by non-native species is projected to increase with higher temperatures, particularly in mid- and high-latitude islands.

Climate Change Has Dangerous Ramifications for Public Health

A. J. McMichael, S. Friel, A. Nyong, and C. Corvalan

A. J. McMichael is a professor and affiliate of the National Centre for Epidemiology and Population Health at Australian National University in Canberra, Australia. S. Friel is a fellow at the National Centre for Epidemiology and Population Health. A. Nyong is director of the Centre for Environmental Resources and Hazards Research in the department of geography and planning at the University of Jos in Nigeria. C. Corvalan is a public health and environment coordinator for the World Health Organization.

Human actions are changing many of the world's natural environmental systems, including the climate system. These systems are intrinsic to life processes and fundamental to human health, and their disruption and depletion make it more difficult to tackle health inequalities. Indeed, we will not achieve the UN millennium development health goals if environmental destruction continues. Health professionals have a vital contributory role in preventing and reducing the health effects of global environmental change.

Problems of Focus

In 2000 the United Nations set out eight development goals to improve the lives of the world's disadvantaged populations. The goals seek reductions in poverty, illiteracy, sex inequality, malnutrition, child deaths, maternal mortality, and major infections as well as creation of environmental stability and a global partnership for development. One problem of this itemisation of goals is that it separates environmental considerations from health

"Global Environmental Change and Health: Impacts, Inequalities, and the Health Sector," by A. J. McMichael, S. Friel, A Nyong, and C. Corvalan, National Center for Biotechnology Information, January 26, 2018.

considerations. Poverty cannot be eliminated while environmental degradation exacerbates malnutrition, disease, and injury. Food supplies need continuing soil fertility, climatic stability, freshwater supplies, and ecological support (such as pollination). Infectious diseases cannot be stabilised in circumstances of climatic instability, refugee flows, and impoverishment.

The seventh millennium development goal also takes a limited view of environmental sustainability, focusing primarily on traditional localised physical, chemical, and microbial hazards. Those hazards, which are associated with industrialisation, urbanisation, and agriculture in lower income countries, remain important as they impinge most on poor and vulnerable communities. Exposure to indoor air pollution, for example, varies substantially between rich and poor in urban and rural populations. And the World Health Organization estimates that a quarter of the global burden of disease, including over one third of childhood burden, is due to modifiable factors in air, water, soil, and food. This estimated environment related burden is much greater in low income than high income countries overall (25% versus 17% of deaths—and widening further to a twofold difference in percentages between the highest and lowest risk countries). Heavy metals and chemical residues contaminate local foods, urban air pollution causes premature deaths, and waterborne enteric pathogens kill two million children annually.

These relatively localised environmental health hazards, though, are mostly remediable. Meanwhile, a larger scale, less remediable, and potentially irreversible category of environmental health hazard is emerging. Human pressures on the natural environment, reflecting global population growth and intensified economic activities, are now so great that many of the world's biophysical and ecological systems are being impaired. Examples of these global environmental changes include climate change, freshwater shortages, loss of biodiversity (with consequent changes to functioning of ecosystems), and exhaustion of fisheries. These changes are unprecedented in scale, and the resultant risks to population health need urgent response by health professionals and the health sector at large.

Who Will Be Affected

The health effects of global environmental change will vary between countries. Loss of healthy life years in low income African countries, for example, is predicted to be 500 times that in Europe. The fourth assessment report of the Intergovernmental Panel on Climate Change concluded that adverse health effects are much more likely in low income countries and vulnerable subpopulations. These disparities may well increase in coming decades, not only because of regional differences in the intensity of environmental changes (such as water shortages and soil erosion), but also because of exacerbations of differentials in economic conditions, levels of social and human capital, political power, and local environmental dependency.

These differential health risks also reflect the wider issue of access to global and local "public goods." Most of the world's arable land has now been privatised; stocks of wild species (fish, animals, and wild plants) are declining as population pressures and commercial activities intensify; and freshwater is increasingly becoming subject to market pricing. Social policies should therefore pay particular attention to the health inequalities that flow from unequal access to environmental fundamentals.

Availability of safe drinking water illustrates the point about access to what, historically, was common property: 1.1 billion people lack safe drinking water, and 2.6 billion lack basic sanitation. Beyond diarrhoeal disease, water related health risks also arise from chemical contamination—such as arsenic as a cause of skin pigmentation, hyperkeratosis, cardiovascular disease, neuropathy, and cancer.

Role of Social Conditions

The relation of environmental impoverishment to health risks and inequalities is complex. Environmental degradation impairs health, while health deficits (for example, malnutrition or depletion of the workforce from AIDS) can amplify environmental mismanagement. This causes inequalities in both health endangering exposures and health outcomes.

India provides a good example of the complexity of these relations. The country's average life expectancy is relatively low but is expected to improve with industrialisation and modernisation. Industrialisation is contributing to the rapid increase of coal burning in India, and the resultant addition to global emissions and climate change amplifies health risks worldwide. These health risks will affect the world's most vulnerable populations.

The risks to population health from environmental change have far reaching implications for prevention strategies. Global changes result in loss of natural resources. Resolution of these risks therefore requires a different approach from that used for the more familiar challenges presented by time limited and reversible local environmental contamination.

Climate Change and Health

Human induced global climate change is now an acknowledged reality. We have taken a long time to recognise the resultant health risks, current and future, and their unequal effects around the world, but the topic is now attracting much attention. Risks to health will arise by direct and indirect pathways and will reflect changes in both average climate conditions and in climatic variability. The main risks are:

- Effects of heat waves and other extreme events (cyclones, floods, storms, wildfires)
- Changes in patterns of infectious disease
- Effects on food yields
- Effects on freshwater supplies
- Impaired functioning of ecosystems (for example, wetlands as water filters)
- Displacement of vulnerable populations (for example, low lying island and coastal populations)
- Loss of livelihoods

Extreme weather events, infection, and malnutrition will have the greatest health effects in poor and vulnerable populations. In sub-Saharan Africa over 110 million people currently live in regions prone to malaria epidemics. Climate change could add 20-70 million to this figure by the 2080s (assuming no population increase, and including forecast malaria reductions in West Africa from drying). Any such increase would exacerbate poverty and make it harder to achieve and sustain health improvements.

Some links between climate change and human health are complex. For example, the predicted drying in sub-Saharan Africa could increase the incidence of HIV infection, as impoverished rural farming families move to cities where conditions foster sex work and unsafe sex.

The recent report of the Global Environmental Change and Human Health project gives a good summary of the major categories of current and predicted health effects of global environmental changes other than climate change.

Africa and Climate Change

Africa is very vulnerable to climate change because of other environmental and social stresses. The economy depends critically on agriculture, which accounts for two thirds of the workforce and up to half of household incomes and food.

- Climate models predict regional increases in mean temperatures of several degrees centigrade by 2100, a decline in summer rainfall in southern and northern Africa and some increase in west and east Africa. Drying, plus the demands of population growth and economic development, will exacerbate regional water scarcity.
- Falls in crop yields due to 1-2°C warming by 2050 would add an estimated 12 million additional Africans to the 200 million currently undernourished.
- Extreme events such as flooding change will affect food availability by damaging roads, storage, and markets—floods in 2000 in Mozambique damaged about 10% of farmland and

90% of irrigation, displaced two million people, and affected up to 1.5 million livelihoods (mostly in poor rural areas).

- Livestock viral diseases such as east coast fever, foot and mouth disease, blue tongue virus, and Rift valley fever are climate sensitive. Regional increases in temperature and rainfall could affect tsetse fly habitat and hence trypanosomiasis in livestock.
- Climate change and agricultural downturn in Africa may force populations to move, generating conflicts over territory. Pastoralists forced to search for grazing land because of wells drying up may partly explain the Darfur crisis in Sudan.

Roles for Doctors and Other Health Professionals

The spectrum of potential strategies to reduce health risks is wide, commensurate with the diversity of threats to health posed by climate change and other global environmental changes. Local policies and actions, both to mitigate environmental change at source and to adapt to existing and unavoidable risks to health, will often need support from health attuned policies at provincial, national, and international levels. For example, community programmes to mosquito-proof houses will need to be reinforced by improvements in the national surveillance of infectious diseases and in outbreak warning systems.

Doctors and other health professionals have particular knowledge, opportunity, and, often, political leverage that can help ensure—through advocacy or direct participation—that preventive actions are taken. Actions include promoting public understanding, monitoring and reporting the health effects of environmental change, and proposing and advocating local adaptive responses.

Various websites list and discuss actions for doctors to take, both individually and collectively. For example, the US Centers for Disease Control and Prevention lists 11 functions for the public health system and practitioners for responding to climate change. And Doctors for the Environment Australia has run a successful, continuing, national campaign of patient education by distributing posters and pamphlets for use in doctors' waiting rooms.

How Health Professionals Can Promote Adaptive Strategies

- Public education, especially through healthcare settings such as doctors' waiting rooms and hospital clinics
- Preventive programmes—eg, vaccines, mosquito control, food hygiene and inspection, nutritional supplementation
- Health care (especially mental health and primary care) for communities affected by environmental adversity
- Surveillance of disease (especially infectious disease) and key risk factors
- Forecasting future health risks from projected climate change
- Forecasting future health risks and gains from mitigation and adaptation strategies
- Health sector workforce training and in-career development

Strategies that extend beyond health sector:

- Early warning systems for impending extreme weather (eg, heat waves, storms)
- Neighbourhood support schemes to protect the most vulnerable people
- Climate-proofed housing design, urban planning, water catchment, and farming practices
- Disaster preparedness, including capacity of the health system

Adaptive Strategies to Lessen Health Risks

Many local actions can be taken to reduce the vulnerability of communities and populations. These will vary considerably between different regions of the world, and in relation to prevailing socioeconomic conditions and available resources. During Australia's recent prolonged drought (2001-7), some rural health doctors reported that fostering and supporting communal activities (community choirs, social gatherings, financial advisory networks, etc) increased local resilience against depression associated with loss of livelihood.

Climate change and other large scale environmental changes are unlikely to cause entirely new diseases (although they may contribute to the emergence of new strains of viruses and other microbes that can infect humans). Rather, they will alter the incidence, range, and seasonality of many existing health disorders. Hence, existing healthcare and public health systems should provide an appropriate starting point for adaptive strategies to lessen health effects.

Preventative Action

Although adaptive strategies will minimise the effects of climate change, the greater public health preventive challenge lies in stopping the process of climate change. This requires bold and far sighted policy decisions at national and international levels, entailing much greater emissions cuts than were being proposed a decade ago.

Scientists have concluded that we need to prevent atmospheric carbon dioxide concentrations exceeding 450-500 ppm to avoid the serious, perhaps irreversible, damage to many natural systems and ecological processes that a global average temperature increase of 2-3°C would cause. This requires early radical action as today's concentrations are approaching 390 ppm (compared with 280 ppm before industrialisation). Health professionals, acting through citizens' or professional organisations, have both the opportunity and responsibility to contribute to resolving this momentous issue. Improving awareness of the problem is the first step. Since 1993, doctors from 14 countries (including six low income countries) have had a central role in the Intergovernmental Panel on Climate Change's assessment of the health effects of climate change. We should also add this topic, including its relevance to health professional activity, to the medical curriculum.

The health sector, meanwhile, must minimise greenhouse gas emissions from its own infrastructure, especially hospitals. Health researchers should act to minimise greenhouse gas emissions from their own studies.

Conclusion

The Stern report, in 2006, highlighted the potentially great damage to the world's economic system from unconstrained climate change. The greater risk, however, is to the vitality and health of all species, including humans, if current trends continue to weaken the earth's life support systems. The health professions have a crucial role in promoting public understanding of this fundamental association and health protecting responses to it

Climate Change Leads to More Severe Weather, Threatening Populations Around the World

Union of Concerned Scientists

The Union of Concerned Scientists is a nonprofit advocacy group representing scientists and public citizens concerned about science-related issues.

From heat waves to hurricanes, heavy rain to severe drought, people across the United States regularly confront the negative effects of extreme weather events—and the cost of these events is increasing. Of the 20 costliest weather and climate disasters that have occurred in the United States since 1980, eight have taken place since 2010, and four of these eight in 2017 alone. In total, extreme events occurring in the United States since 1980 have resulted in nearly 10,000 deaths and more than $1.6 trillion in damage, according to official estimates, though these estimates likely undercount deaths.

As the economic and human toll of extreme weather events has grown, so too has our understanding of the role climate change plays in worsening many types of extreme events. Over the past decade, the scientific field known as "climate attribution" has developed rapidly as scientists have been increasingly able to identify and quantify the part human-driven climate change plays in increasing the frequency and intensity of many types of extreme weather events.

In a landmark 2004 paper, researchers determined that climate change had at least doubled the risk of occurrence of the record-breaking 2003 European summer heat wave, which resulted in the deaths of tens of thousands of people. A 2016 study of the same heat wave concluded that human-caused climate change had

"Is Global Warming Linked to Severe Weather?" Union of Concerned Scientists, June 2018. Reprinted by permission.

increased the risk of heat-related mortality during the event by about 70 percent in central Paris and about 20 percent in London.

Numerous authoritative scientific institutions and government agencies have released studies in recent years that reflect how much the science of climate attribution has developed:

- The *Bulletin of the American Meteorological Society* has dedicated a special issue each year since 2012 to assessing whether and how much climate change may have contributed to extreme weather events. The 2016 special issues states, "The science has now advanced to the point that we can detect the effects of climate change on some events with high confidence."
- The National Academies of Sciences, Engineering, and Medicine issued a report in 2016, *Attribution of Extreme Weather Events in the Context of Climate Change*, that states, "In the past, a typical climate scientist's response to questions about climate change's role in any given extreme weather event was, 'We cannot attribute any single event to climate change.' The science has advanced to the point that this is no longer true as an unqualified blanket statement."
- The US Global Change Research Program released the first volume of the *Fourth National Climate Assessment, the Climate Science Special Report*, in November 2016. The report states this key finding: "The attribution of extreme weather and climate events has been an emerging area in the science of detection and attribution. Attribution of extreme weather events under a changing climate is now an important and highly visible aspect of climate science."

Strength of the Evidence

Strong evidence suggests that extreme heat waves, coastal flooding resulting from storm surge and regular high-tide events, and extreme precipitation—including hurricane downpours—bear a strong climate change signature. Scientists are better able to identify climate change's relative contribution for these types of extreme weather events than for others. The science is currently less conclusive for tornados, thunderstorms, and some types of droughts, and there is growing evidence for wildfires.

In the case of wildfires, a combination of factors influences risk. Those tied to human-caused climate changes, such as warming temperatures and drying soils, have contributed to observed increases in wildfire activity—area burned, the number of large wildfires, and wildfire season length—in the western United States in recent decades. It is important to note, however, that factors unrelated to climate change, including land use and fire suppression practices, also affect wildfire risk. In southern California, for example, while climate change plays a role, development and seasonal Santa Ana winds also contribute to increased wildfire activity. However, in high elevation forests where there has been minimal human activity, climate change plays a greater role.

An extreme weather event's intensity is another important factor for determining whether climate change played a role. While many individual extreme events could have occurred in the past, before the advent of human-caused climate change, they likely would not have been as intense without its influence. Recent studies find that some record-breaking heat events were so extreme that they would have been nearly or entirely impossible if it were not for human influence on the climate system.

Individual Event Attribution

Over the past several years, scientists have been able to discern the influence of climate change on individual extreme weather events, including heat waves, extreme precipitation and flooding events, droughts, and extreme cold snaps, as well as on the intensity of hurricanes.

When scientists investigate climate change's effects on extreme events, they are not asking whether climate change caused an event. Instead, they attempt to determine whether and by how much climate change has affected the likelihood or intensity of an event. They often rely on real-world observations incorporated into climate models, which make calculations to simulate what would likely happen if individual conditions—such as global average temperatures—were different.

Extreme events are by definition rate—if they occurred regularly, we would likely not consider them extreme. By running climate models that recreate real-world condition at the time of an event, scientists can determine just how rare—that is, how likely or unlikely—an event that actually occurred really was. Researchers then determine the likelihood of the same event under a different set of conditions by repeating the process using a climate model that simulates a hypothetical world in which humans have no influence on the climate. By comparing the likelihoods under these two scenarios, researchers can determine the extent to which human-caused climate change affected an event.

Recent US extreme weather events that scientists have tied to climate change include:

- Hurricane Harvey (August 2017): Human-caused climate change made the record rainfall that hit Houston during Hurricane Harvey roughly three times more likely and 15 percent more intense.
- US winter heat wave (February 2017): Human-caused climate change made the heat wave that spread across the contiguous United States in February 2017 more than three times more likely.
- Louisiana floods (August 2016): Human-caused climate change increased the likelihood of the extreme rain event that hit Louisiana on August 2, 2016, by at least 40 percent.
- Hurricane Sandy (October 2012): Hurricane Sandy's storm surge—already made more damaging by the exceptionally high lunar tides—flooded an area about 27 square miles larger than it would have if the storm had hit in 1880 because human-caused climate change has caused global mean sea levels to rise by eight inches since then.

Increased Risk, Increased Understanding

Climate attribution science is filling critical gaps in our understanding of the connection between extreme weather and climate change. This increased understanding presents an opportunity to determine whether the ways we currently plan for, respond to, and recover from extreme weather events are appropriate for a world where climate change makes many types of extreme events worse. Ensuring that we are fully aware of the risks posed by climate change when we make individual and institutional decisions about disaster planning offers us the best chance to protect livelihoods, homes, and communities.

Climate Change Impacts Food Security

Food and Agricultural Organization of the United Nations

The Food and Agricultural Organization of the United Nations (FAO) oversees international research and initiatives surrounding food security.

[...]

This chapter presents the breadth and scope of disaster impact on the agriculture sector. Key global trends for damage and losses to the agriculture sector are presented, followed by a discussion of the nature of disaster impact on agriculture subsectors (crops, livestock, fisheries and forestry) and natural resources, with trends in damage and losses for each. The wider impact of disasters is then presented across the value chain, on agro-industries, national economies, livelihoods and food security, as well as the cumulative damage and losses caused by recurring disasters.

Global Trends in Damage and Losses to the Agriculture Sector

Overall Damage and Losses to Agriculture

FAO analysed the damage and losses to the agriculture sector caused by 78 disaster events that occurred between 2003 and 2013 in developing countries in Africa, Asia and the Pacific, and Latin America and the Caribbean. These included small-, medium- and large-scale disasters, 13 of which occurred in Africa, 27 in Asia and the Pacific, 37 in Latin America and the Caribbean, and one in Eastern Europe.

The data analysed is based on information reported in needs assessments, which are typically undertaken in the immediate aftermath of disasters as a collaborative effort between governments

"The Impact of Disasters on Agriculture and Food Security," Food and Agriculture Organization of the United Nations. Reprinted by permission.

and the international community to assess the impact of a disaster on all major affected sectors. The study calculated the damage and losses to the agriculture sector as reported in these needs assessments. In the assessments, damage refers to the total or partial destruction of physical assets and infrastructure in the affected areas in terms of their monetary value expressed as replacement costs. Losses refer to the changes in economic flows arising from the disaster and that continue until economic recovery is achieved.

Together, the 78 disasters cost USD 30 billion in damage and losses to agriculture and its subsectors, out of a total of USD 140 billion in combined damage and losses across all sectors.

Disasters have an impact across a range of sectors depending on their magnitude, geographic location and other characteristics. The reviewed needs assessments typically evaluated the damage and losses to productive sectors such as agriculture, livelihoods, commerce and industry, commerce and trade, and tourism; to social sectors such as housing, education, health, culture and nutrition; and to infrastructure such as water and sanitation, energy and electricity, transport and telecommunications.

The damage and losses calculated for the agriculture sector were analysed in relation to the damage and losses to all sectors combined, expressed in terms of the percentage share of the total. The findings indicate that in terms of direct physical damage alone, roughly 14 percent was to the agriculture sector while the remaining damage was to other sectors.

This direct damage to agriculture typically includes the partial or total destruction of vital agricultural infrastructure and assets, including standing crops; farm tools and equipment; irrigation systems; livestock shelters and veterinary services; fishing boats and equipment; landing sites; aquaculture equipment and hatcheries; post-production infrastructure such as storage, processing, marketing and transport facilities; buildings and equipment of farm schools and cooperatives, and sector ministries and their departments, among others.

Of all the indirect losses these disasters caused, nearly 30 percent was to the agriculture sector alone. In other words, the greatest economic impact of disasters to the agriculture sector stems from losses, while the physical damage is comparatively smaller given the relatively lower monetary value of agricultural assets when compared with infrastructure such as housing or roads. The losses to the agriculture sector may include a decline in output in crop, livestock, fisheries and aquaculture, and forestry production; increased cost of production from higher outlays on farm inputs such as fertilizers, seeds, livestock feed and veterinary care, among others; lower revenues and higher operational costs in the provision of services; and unexpected expenditures to meet humanitarian and recovery needs in the sector.

When damage and losses are combined, the agriculture sector absorbs an average of 22 percent of the total impact of natural hazards—a figure much higher than previously reported. The remaining damage and losses are to other sectors such as housing, health, education, transport and communication, electricity, water and sanitation, commerce, industry, tourism, and the environment, among others. When considering only climate-related disasters —such as floods, droughts, hurricanes, typhoons and cyclones (excluding geological hazards such as earthquakes, tsunamis and volcanic eruptions)—the percentage share of the total damage and losses affecting agriculture rises. Twenty-five percent of the economic impact caused by climate-related disasters falls on the agriculture sector.

However, the percentage share of damage and losses to the agriculture sector varies significantly among the disasters analysed, influenced by the type of disaster, their magnitude or specific geographic location (rural versus urban), among other factors. For example, in Kenya, 85 percent of all damage and losses caused by drought between 2008 and 2011 were to the agriculture sector. In Pakistan, the sector suffered roughly 50 percent of the total economic impact of the 2010 floods, while tropical storm O3B which struck Yemen in 2008 inflicted 63 percent of its impact on the agriculture sector, and the Indonesian tsunami in 2004 almost 20 percent.

The data was analysed by type of disaster to determine which caused the greatest damage and losses to agriculture, expressed as the percentage share of total damage and losses to all sectors combined. The findings show that of all natural hazards, the relationship between drought and agriculture is particularly important as 84 percent of the damage and losses caused by droughts is to agriculture, while the remaining impact is typically to sectors such as health and nutrition, energy, water and sanitation, among others. This figure is an estimate based on three needs assessments available on droughts – in Djibouti (2008–2011), Kenya (2008–2011) and Uganda (2010–2011). [...] Hurricanes, cyclones, typhoons and floods also have a considerable impact on the agriculture sector, while geological disasters have a comparatively lower economic impact. These findings reveal that a significant proportion of the overall economic impact of disasters falls on the agriculture sector when compared with the total impact on all sectors combined. This is especially true in the case of climate-related disasters, particularly droughts. Yet, there are strong indications that damage and losses to agriculture are considerably higher than reported. For example, the data does not include the damage and losses to agriculture-based small and medium enterprises or on-farm unemployment and the consequent income loss caused by disasters. Such data is typically grouped under a separate "livelihoods" sector in the assessments analysed.

In addition, disaster impact on subsectors such as fisheries and forestry is not always reported in the assessments. More systematic assessments and analyses of disaster impact across sectors are needed to provide guidance for the mainstreaming of disaster risk reduction into development policies and strategies. The large share of drought impact absorbed by agriculture, for example, called for the development of national drought management policies in affected countries.

Regular assessment of damage and losses caused by drought would provide invaluable support to policy-makers for the mainstreaming of drought management principles and actions into agricultural development plans.

Disasters that have a significant impact on agriculture will typically slow down sector growth, as well as national GDP in countries where the sector drives economic growth. Yet these losses are not usually calculated in assessments and are therefore not reflected in the data reported above. Finally, the findings do not reflect losses in agro-industries that result directly from agricultural production losses, such as in the food processing and textile industries which directly depend on agricultural inputs.

Impact of Disasters on the Agriculture Subsectors and Natural Resources

Impact of Disasters on Crops, Livestock, Fisheries and Forestry
A closer analysis was undertaken of the damage and losses caused by the 78 disasters, with respect to each subsector: crops, livestock, fisheries and forestry. The findings show that within the agriculture sector, the crop subsector absorbs over 42 percent of the total damage and losses caused by disasters, while the livestock subsector sustains nearly 34 percent of the total economic impact within agriculture.

Fisheries absorb about 5.5 percent and forestry roughly 2.3 percent of the impact. However, the impact of natural hazards on these two subsectors was not always reported in the assessments analysed, so these findings likely underestimate the actual economic impact of disasters on fisheries and forestry.

At the same time, different types of disasters have a differentiated impact on each subsector, depending on their exposure and vulnerability or their relative importance to national or local economies and livelihoods. For example, crops tend to be most affected by floods and storms; together they account for an estimated 93 percent of the economic impact on the subsector.

Livestock is overwhelmingly affected by droughts, causing nearly 86 percent of all damage and losses to the subsector.

One study found that nine major droughts in selected African countries between 1981 and 2000 resulted in average livestock loss of 40 percent, with a range of 22–90 percent. In Kenya, the livestock subsector was most severely affected during the 2008–2011 drought, which caused USD 9 billion in damage and losses during this period. The drought depleted pastures and water, especially in the arid and semi-arid land areas, resulting in the deterioration of livestock body condition and reduced immunity. This triggered massive migration of livestock to other regions with better water sources, and the congregation of migrating herds led to increased and widespread disease outbreaks in most parts of Kenya. Livestock mortality from starvation and disease affected 9 percent of livestock, while disease incidence reached more than 40 percent of herds in the affected districts.

This has changed livestock composition and usage, and depressed livestock productivity. Livestock migration and reduced productivity caused food insecurity, loss of earnings, separation of families, school dropouts, environmental degradation and resource-based conflicts. In addition, high food prices deteriorated the purchasing capacity of households and the terms of trade for pastoralists (50–60 percent below the five-year average). In arid and semi-arid land districts, pastoralists reported critical rates of acute malnutrition in children (global acute malnutrition >20 percent), falling within the World Health Organization emergency threshold. In 2011, some 3.7 million people were food insecure—1.8 million in marginal agricultural areas and 1.9 million in pastoral areas.

The fisheries subsector is most affected by tsunamis and storms such as hurricanes and cyclones, while most of the economic impact to forestry is caused by floods and storms (excluding wild fires). Of the 78 disasters reviewed, the 2004 tsunami affecting India and Indonesia had the greatest economic impact on fisheries, causing over USD 500 million in damage and losses to the subsector in each country. Fisheries also tend to suffer more in small island developing states. In the Maldives, 70 percent of the economic impact of the 2004 tsunami in the agriculture sector was to fisheries, which had an enormous impact on livelihoods and the national economy. The subsector (fisheries and fish processing) contributed over 9 percent to national GDP in 2004 and was the second major source of foreign exchange after tourism. One-third of the annual catch is typically consumed domestically, while fish accounted for almost half of the country's exports. The sector employed 11 percent of the labour force and about 20 percent of the total population relies on fisheries as their main income-earning activity. Fisheries infrastructure and assets were destroyed or damaged, including fishery island harbours and safe anchorage, boat sheds, fishing vessels, cottage and commercial fish processors and other assets. Within the fisheries subsector, pole and line tuna harvesting and small-scale fish processing were most affected by the tsunami.

In the case of forestry, biomass fires have a significant impact, burning annually between 3 and 4.5 million km^2 globally—an area equivalent to India and Pakistan combined—with negative consequences for the multiple services that forests provide to local ecosystems and the natural capital on which agriculture depends. Cyclone Nargis which struck Myanmar in 2008 caused almost USD 55 million in damage and losses to the forestry subsector. The cyclone also impacted other subsectors. About 2.4 million people were affected, mainly in the country's Ayeyarwady River Delta where 50–60 percent of families are engaged in agriculture and between 20 and 30 percent are landless, relying on fishing and agricultural labour. The cyclone affected paddy crops and plantation crops, and caused the loss of 50 percent of buffaloes and 20 percent of cattle in the worst-affected townships. Over half of small rice mills and two-thirds of larger rice mills in the affected areas were damaged. Commercial intensive aquaculture was affected by the damage to fisheries infrastructure, while heavy damage to both onshore production facilities and fishing boats affected the production of dried fish and shrimp, and fish paste. As a result, the cyclone had a critical impact on livelihoods, employment and income, particularly in the informal sector, such as seasonal jobs in agriculture, community works, small-scale fishing, rice mills, fish processing, salt production, wood cutting, and other resource-based economic activities.

Smallholder farmers lost income-earning opportunities, as did those involved in small-scale inshore and offshore fishing, landless poor dependent on wage labour in agriculture and skilled workers previously employed in a wide range of small and medium manufacturing and processing enterprises.

These findings show how the agriculture subsectors can be affected differently by disasters. Understanding these differences is critical to the formulation of policy and practices at national, subnational and community levels. Measures to strengthen the resilience of marine fisheries, for example, need to consider tsunamis and storms which tend to cause the greatest impact, whereas inland fisheries must consider the impact of floods and droughts. Wild fires and drought (often combined) are important hazards affecting forestry, which require special attention in risk reduction policies and planning.

Furthermore, disaggregated subsectoral data on disaster impact is needed to support the implementation of innovative risk management tools, such as weather risk insurance schemes for agriculture and rural livelihoods. Systematic and coherent data availability will facilitate the design of insurance schemes which would help to further diversify risk mitigation strategies.

Another consideration is the potential contribution that the subsectors can make in post-disaster situations, depending on the relative impact on each. For instance, capture fisheries can be restored relatively quickly after a disaster (provided that no serious damage has been caused to the aquatic environment) and may be able to provide alternative livelihoods to affected populations during the recovery phase. Assessments of disaster impact on each of the subsectors will vary at country and subnational levels, and investments to reduce risk and build resilience in these subsectors should be informed by the particular nature of disaster impact on that subsector.

Yet, forestry and fisheries tend to be under-reported in needs assessments and the impact of disasters on these must be better assessed and understood.

Impacts of Disasters on Natural Resources and Ecosystem Services

Disasters also damage or destroy natural resources and ecosystem services that sustain agriculture. Land, water and biological diversity form the natural resource base of agriculture, essential to rural livelihoods and sustainable agricultural development. For example, forests and tree-based agricultural systems contribute to the livelihoods of an estimated 1 billion people globally. Wild foods are important for food security and nutrition, while trees and forests are vital in the provision of ecosystem services to agriculture. Marine, coastal and inland areas also support a rich assortment of aquatic biodiversity. The planet already faces multiple pressures, including on fragile soils, water supplies, competing demands for land, over fishing and other pressures, and the impact of disasters further erodes this vital resource base for agriculture and livelihoods.

Disasters contribute to ecosystem degradation and loss, including increased soil erosion, declining rangeland quality, salinization of soils, deforestation and biodiversity loss. Increasing environmental degradation reduces the availability of goods and services to local communities, shrinks economic opportunities and livelihood options, and ultimately contributes to greater food insecurity and hunger. It further drives increasing numbers of people to use marginal lands and fragile environments.

Yet, the impact of disasters on natural resources and the environment is not always evaluated in needs assessments and remains a largely under-assessed sector, in terms of direct and indirect economic losses. However, some trends can be observed from the 78 disasters reviewed, which show that 43 of these disasters affected natural resources and the environment, causing over USD 2.3 billion in damage and losses.

In 2007, Hurricane Felix in Nicaragua caused a total of USD 552 million in damage and losses to natural resources and the environment, in addition to USD 57 million in damage and losses to the agriculture sector. Tropical Storm Agatha and the volcanic eruption of Pacaya in 2010 in Guatemala also had a considerable impact on the sector, causing USD 260 million in damage and losses.

At the same time, the deforestation caused by disasters and their degradation of land, catchments and watersheds, depletion of reefs and coastal ecosystems such as corals and mangroves, reduce nature's defense capacity against future hazards. Forests serve as shelterbelts and windbreaks, and protect against landslides, floods and avalanches. Trees stabilize riverbanks and mitigate soil erosion, while woodlots provide fuel wood, timber and fodder. Forests are estimated to save between USD 2 billion and USD 3.5 billion per year equivalent in disaster damage restoration of key forest ecosystems.

Wider and Cumulative Impact of Disasters

Assessments of the impact of disasters on the agriculture sector apply different approaches and methodologies. Some focus on the economic impact, such as the needs assessments reviewed in the previous sections which evaluate damage and losses. However, these do not assess the cascading and wider impact that disasters have on the food value chain, agro-industries and sector growth, or capture the implications for livelihoods and food security. Some assessments do follow a livelihoods approach or focus on food security. These and other types of assessments represent different analytical lenses through which we can measure impact, yielding different results. The approaches and findings they produce are complementary; together they present a holistic picture of disaster impact on agriculture and its broader consequences.

The wider impact of disasters on the agriculture sector as a whole and its potential consequences are grouped into six core categories:

- Direct physical damage
- Losses across the food value chain (backward-forward linkages)
- Losses to manufacturing (agro-industries)
- Consequent macro-economic impact
- Impact on livelihoods, food security and nutrition
- Effect on sustainable development

This section presents an overview of the broader impact based on case studies.

The physical damage caused by disasters has a direct impact on agricultural production with negative consequences along the food value chain, including backward linkages—disrupting the flow of agricultural inputs such as seeds and fertilizers—and forward linkages with processing and distribution, markets and retailers. Disasters can destroy the infrastructure of input suppliers and post-harvest facilities. They can interrupt food supply, market access and trade. In medium- and large-scale disasters, high production losses can lead to increases in imports of food and agricultural commodities to compensate for lost production and meet domestic demand, increasing public expenditure. They can also reduce exports and revenues, with negative consequences for the balance of payment. When post-disaster production losses are significant and in countries where the sector makes an important contribution to economic growth, agriculture value-added or sector growth falls, as does national GDP.

In addition, the agriculture sector supplies vital resources to industry and stimulates the growth of some manufacturing subsectors. Therefore, agricultural production losses can reduce manufacturing/industrial output in sectors that depend on agriculture and raw materials. Agro-industries such as food processing are particularly vulnerable. In some cases, non-food agro-industries, such as the textile industry, can also be negatively affected by production losses. Such agro-industries (both food and non-food) will suffer from losses in production as well, with similar consequences for domestic supplies, exports, national revenues and ultimately manufacturing value added. The inter-dependence between agriculture and industry is important to the economies of least developed countries where agro-industrial sectors account for two-thirds of the manufacturing output. The share of agro-industrial sectors in total manufacturing value added is 70 percent in United Republic of Tanzania, 51 percent in Ethiopia, 35 percent in Kenya, 29 percent in Mexico and 20 percent in India.

At the same time, disasters directly impact on agricultural livelihoods, food security and nutrition. Disasters can cause unemployment and/or a decline in wages and therefore income among farmers and farm labourers, and lower the availability of food commodities in local markets which typically produces food inflation. Such pressures reduce the purchasing capacity of households, restrict access to food, deplete savings, force the sale of vital productive assets, increase indebtedness and erode livelihoods.

Ultimately, the quantity and quality of food consumption is reduced, and food insecurity and malnutrition increases, particularly among the most vulnerable households. This impact is most felt at the local and household levels in disaster-affected areas.

The extent to which disasters erode livelihoods, produce food insecurity, cause disruptions along the food value chain, reduce manufacturing output and lower sector growth and national GDP varies depending on numerous factors beyond the study's scope.

Such factors include the nature, location and scale of the disaster; its timing in relation to the agricultural calendar; the size and composition of the agriculture sector; its relative importance to employment, income, manufacturing and national GDP; the vulnerability of the sector and affected populations to shocks; and the emergency policies or measures introduced by governments to mitigate the impact of disasters.

In sub-Saharan Africa, for example, droughts cause significant damage and losses to agriculture. In Uganda, the 2005–2007 drought and 2010–2011 rainfall deficits had far-reaching impacts on the national economy, causing production losses especially for the livestock subsector, reducing exports, affecting agro-industries and slowing the GDP growth rate.

In many countries, disasters are frequent events that over time incur a high economic cost in total damage and losses, as well as in repeated investments in recovery by governments and the international community. A significant number of developing countries experience recurring disasters. Over the last decade, more than one-third of all developing countries have been affected by at least three medium- and large-scale disasters. The most affected countries were Ethiopia, which faced six reported droughts, and India with six reported floods. The cumulative impact of several disasters on the agriculture sector is illustrated by the examples from the Philippines, Pakistan and Mexico.

[…]

One important element not typically considered in the analysis of disaster impact on the agriculture sector is the consequences on other sectors that are closely linked and depend on agriculture, such as food and non-food agro-industries. This needs to be better assessed and understood given that they account for the bulk of manufacturing output in many less-developed countries. Understanding the full ramifications of disasters is essential for countries to formulate well-designed and tailored strategies that can effectively buffer or mitigate the high cost to national economic growth.

[…]

Technology Is Providing New Ways to Combat Climate Change and Environmental Catastrophe

Lyndsey Gilpin

Lyndsey Gilpin is the founder and editor-in-chief of Southerly, *a media organization about ecology, justice, and culture in the southern United States.*

Astartling new report on climate change was released in early 2014. It didn't mention exact dates or specific forecasts for the future, but it did foreshadow consequences of climate change that are getting increasingly difficult for the world to ignore.

Some of the highlights included a prediction of violent conflicts and civil wars, extreme poverty and the loss of several points of gross domestic product in some developing nations, mass extinctions, and an intense, regular pattern of natural disasters.

The report was done by the Intergovernmental Panel on Climate Change, a United Nations group that summarizes the effects of climate change every so often. The year 2013 is tied with 2003 as the fourth warmest year on record for planet earth, and the top 10 have all been since 1998.

From automobiles to factories, technology has played its part in climate change. But, tech can also change the course we're on, if it's harnessed in effective ways. Here are 10 creative ways humans are using technology to fight climate change.

Big Data

Big data has big implications in creating awareness about the consequences of climate change. The UN just announced a global competition—the Big Data Climate Challenge—to spur the use

"10 Ways Technology Is Fighting Climate Change," by Lyndsey Gilpin, CBS Interactive, August 6, 2014. Used with permission of TechRepublic.com. Copyright © 2019 CBS Interactive. All rights reserved.

of big data to tackle the issue. It seeks recently published projects that show the economic impact of climate change patterns. The contest is part of the Climate Summit in September.

Mobile Apps

It takes some digging to find apps that will help you create real change on a daily basis, but they're out there. Here are some examples of apps that can help you monitor and reduce your carbon footprint and waste.

- Oroeco is an app that tracks your carbon footprint by placing a carbon value on everything you buy, eat, and do, and then shows you how you compare with your neighbors.
- PaperKarma is an easy way to cut paper waste. Take a photo of your junk mail, send it through the app, and PaperKarma will figure out what it is and take you off the mailing list.
- GiveO2 tracks your carbon footprint as you travel. Turn on the tracker when you start a new trip, and it will automatically calculate a timeline of your carbon usage. At the end, you can "offset" it by supporting a sustainable project of your choice.

Hackathons

Hackathons are powerful tools, and they're becoming more mainstream. Companies, organizations, and governments are all using the events to generate fresh ideas. Crowdsourcing for environmental solutions by gathering journalists, scientists, technologists, and people passionate about sustainability is creating a new wave of environmentalism. The White House is now hosting green hackathons of their own.

Clean Energy

Clean energy is perhaps the biggest issue to tackle, but also the most important. In 2013, renewable energy accounted for 10% of total US energy usage and 13% of electricity generation, according to the US Energy and Information Administration. Solar power accounted for only 0.3% of the US energy supply in 2013. Wind energy accounted for 4%.

Some of the biggest challenges for clean energy are storage and transmission of the energy once it's captured. That's where tech comes in to help build a smarter energy grid, which can have nearly as big of an impact on the use of renewable energy sources as new breakthroughs in science.

IoT

Monitoring our energy usage makes it possible to be smarter about it. Take Nest for instance. While an unprogrammed thermostat can waste 20% of heating and cooling, Nest tackles the issue with a smart thermostat that learns your patterns and automatically adjusts to save energy. The Internet of Things can save energy and carbon footprints with things as simple as using an app to turn off the lights or with apps like IFTTT, which hooks up to many different types of systems. The IoT can also involve monitoring your sprinkler system to save water, or use sensors to tell you to take a different route when driving to avoid idling in traffic and wasting gas.

Meat Replacements

The livestock industry is a massive contributor to climate change. It takes more power to make one burger than to fully power seven iPads. Beef alone requires 28 times more land to produce than pork or chicken, 11 times more water and has five times more climate-warming emissions, which estimates to a fifth of total emissions, according to a new paper published by Bard College, the Weizmann Institute of Science, and Yale University.

Technology is making it easier to cut out the animal-based foods. Startups are trying to tackle these issues. Hampton Creek is making egg-free substitutes for cookie dough and mayonnaise, with plans to do much more in the future. Beyond Meat is a plant protein that looks and tastes like meat. Modern Meadow uses tissue engineering to make leather and meat products.

Open Source Movement

Open data and open source technologies are a huge way to accelerate environmental research and innovation. Take Tesla, for example. By opening the company's patents to everyone, Elon Musk wanted to make sure electric vehicles succeed faster. The US government just opened all their climate data to the public to make it easier to access and digest. There's even been talks of open source GMO development, to take the decisions out of the hands of companies like Monsanto and give power to smaller biotech companies with smart ideas to feed the world.

Mapping

It's a simple technology, but interactive maps really drive home the point of climate change. If people can see how vast the world is and how differently certain areas are affected by sea level rise and a warming climate through maps, the science behind it makes more sense. Last month, the US Geological Survey launched a $13 million 3D Elevation Program to develop advanced mapping to better update flood maps and find out where the best areas for solar and wind farms.

Geoengineering

Geoengineering is a controversial method, sometimes called "planet hacking" because it uses literal hacking of the planet's resources to find new solutions. It's based on the belief climate change can be halted using man-made means. It usually takes the form of two things: carbon dioxide reduction, like building algae farms, planting trees, capturing emissions from power stations for fuel; or, solar radiation management, like releasing volcanic ash as a coolant, arranging mirrors in space to redirect solar rays, or painting roofs white instead of black. It's controversial because we don't know the environmental or health effects of most of these ideas.

Data Centers

Apple now boasts that it uses 100% renewable energy in their data centers—especially aided by the largest private solar array in the United States. Google is moving toward that goal as well, though they use 34% right now. It's a good move, because much of the energy used in data centers is not from the actual technology, but from cooling the servers. One study said data centers contributed 1.5% of overall energy usage, so using renewables instead could make a dent.

Cities Can Work with Private Companies to Enable Innovation in Mitigating Environmental Catastrophe

Christopher Cadham

Christopher Cadham is a research associate for the Lombardi Comprehensive Cancer Center at Georgetown University.

Following the climate talks in Paris this past December, there has been increased focus on steps being taken by individual cities to fight climate change. In a Dec. 4 post on this blog, we outlined the steps a number of cities are taking. Many of these cities are outperforming their nation; New York is a prime example.

At the Paris climate talks (known as "COP21," the Conference of Parties to the UN's climate change efforts), New York was given the Building Energy Efficiency award by the C40 Cities Climate Leadership Group, a network of the world's megacities committed to addressing climate change, for its One City: Built to Last program. This aggressive program seeks to cut New York's carbon emissions from buildings by 30 percent of 2005 levels by 2025 and 80 percent by 2050.

Why are buildings so important? In a city as large and densely populated as New York, buildings account for almost three quarters of New York's contribution to climate change. Vast amounts of energy go toward heating, cooling and lighting these buildings, many of which lack high standards of efficiency. In order to effectively reduce the city's carbon footprint, it is vital to not only provide green sources of power and heat for all of these buildings, but also to retrofit buildings to ensure that energy flows through them efficiently.

One City: Built to Last outlines the city's plan to retrofit all city-owned buildings with a significant energy usage within the next

"NYC's Public-Private Partnerships to Fight Climate Change," by Christopher Cadham, Earth Institute Columbia University, March 30, 2016. Reprinted by permission.

10 years. This would mean working on some 3,000 out of the 4,000-plus buildings the city owns. While the report outlines beneficial strides the city is making to improve the energy efficiency of its buildings, New York City has almost one million buildings, the vast majority of which are not owned by the city. It is important to note that not all of these buildings have extensive energy usage. But, it illustrates that solely retrofitting city-owned buildings would come nowhere near the goal of 80 percent reductions by 2050. In order to meet these goals, the city is relying on its Carbon Challenge, an effort to get private and institutional organizations on board to reduce their greenhouse gas emissions by 30 percent in 10 years.

The largest contributors to the city's carbon emissions are residential and commercial buildings. While the city continues to raise the construction code standards, this has limited effect on buildings already standing, 85 percent of which are expected to still be standing by 2030. Therefore, not only is the plan to retrofit buildings crucial to any attempt to cut emissions in this city, but so is fostering public and private partnerships in order to tackle climate change.

Prior to COP21, the Urban Climate Change Research Network, a consortium of over 600 researchers, released their Summary For City Leaders report on Climate Change and Cities. This report outlines the importance of encouraging private sector partnerships into engagement rather than just mere investment. These partnerships that can help to advance innovation, capacity building and institutional leadership "are necessary for effective action," the report says. In the context of cities, these partnership become even more valuable. This is because climate actions on the city level tend to be dominated by smaller scale, incremental changes that are brought on by community actions, local institutions and private actors.

The mayor's office projects that *One City: Built to Last,* which includes the Carbon Challenge, will reduce greenhouse gas emission by 3.4 million metric tons a year by 2025—the equivalent to taking 715,000 vehicles off the road. It will also generate cost-savings across the public and private sectors of more than $1.4 billion a year by 2025, leading to $8.5 billion in cumulative energy cost-savings over 10 years. The city's report anticipates the creation of 3,500 new jobs in construction and energy services, in addition to the training of more than 7,000 building staff to upgrade their skills.

Thus far 17 universities, 11 hospital organizations, 11 global companies, an alliance of 40 Broadway theaters and 18 residential management firms have taken up the challenge. Five universities, one hospital, and two commercial offices have already achieved the 30 percent goal.

The Carbon Challenge, by working to build these partnerships, is helping to move New York City toward its goal of 80 percent emissions reductions by 2050. As the largest city to commit to such a goal, New York City acts as a leader in fighting climate change. If effective, this public-private partnership model might demonstrate to other cities what can be done to reach their targets. With the first deadlines of the challenge approaching it will be fascinating to see the steps that private partners are taking to cut their emissions.

Adaptation Itself Will Require Changes to Our Way of Life

National Climate Change Adaptation Research Facility

The National Climate Change Adaptation Research Facility (NCCARF) is an Australian organization that explores ways the government can adapt and respond to climate change.

D espite international efforts to reduce emissions of greenhouse gases, climate change is likely to have significant effects on coastal Australia. These effects, which include sea-level rise and changes in the occurrence of extreme events, have the potential to significantly impact the livelihoods and lifestyles of coastal residents and the natural environment. Decisions and actions that help to prepare for the adverse consequences of climate change, as well as to take advantage of the opportunities, are known as *climate change adaptation.*

Climate changes on all timescales from short-term fluctuations such as El Niño events through to glacial-interglacial fluctuations lasting many thousands of years. Humans, and the environment in which we live, have adapted to these changes.

Emissions of greenhouse gases from human activities are just one cause of climate change. These excess emissions are already causing our climate to change, and will continue to have effects several centuries into the future. We are already adapting to these changes and will continue to adapt in the future. However, the rate of change is high and at the moment increasing—this challenges the ability of both human and natural systems to "keep up"—to adapt sufficiently quickly to avoid negative impacts.

"What Is Adaptation to Climate Change?" National Climate Change Adaptation Research Facility, May 2, 2017. Reproduced by kind permission of the National Climate Change Adaptation Research Facility, Griffith University, Queensland, Australia.

Adaptation can happen at any level in society from the individual up to national and international levels. In general, the higher up you go, the more the adaptation responses tend to be policies that frame action at lower levels.

Not all the effects of climate change will be negative, and this is especially true in the early years of warming. However, adaptation may be required to realise any positive benefits. In the coastal zone, for example, tourism may benefit if the climate of rival international beach holiday destinations becomes unpleasantly hot. Adaptations such as improvements to tourism infrastructure, e.g. hotel capacity, will be required to fully realise this potential benefit. As climate change progresses through the twenty-first century and beyond, the likelihood of any beneficial effects will diminish.

The ability to adapt is known as adaptive capacity. *Adaptive capacity* is defined by the IPCC (2014) as the "ability of systems, institutions, humans, and other organisms to adjust to potential damage, to take advantage of opportunities, or to respond to consequences." The important word here is "ability"—just because there is the capacity to do something does not necessarily translate into action. Thus, Australia has high capacity to adapt—it is relatively affluent, with robust institutions and a well-educated and healthy population. But that capacity does not necessarily translate into action to address the risks of climate change.

Definitions of "Types" of Adaptation

A literature has grown up around different types of adaptation and their definition. Note that an adaptation action can combine different types—for example, it can include both incremental and public.

Incremental: A series of relatively small actions and adjustments aimed at continuing to meet the existing goals and expectations of the community in the face of the impacts of climate change. *Example: Beach nourishment to maintain the current shoreline and beach quality, and avoid damage to houses on the sea-front, in the face of sea-level rise.*

Transformational: Adaptation actions which result in a significant change to community goals and expectations, or how they are met, potentially disrupting those communities and their values. Transformational adaptation is generally undertaken when incremental adaptation is no longer sufficient to address the risks. *Example: Relocation of an entire suburb or community including homes, businesses and infrastructure, and abandonment of sea-front houses.*

Anticipatory or proactive: Adaptation that takes place before the impacts of climate change are observed. *Example: Local government prevents new development on a greenfield site located in an area likely to be inundated during high tides in 50 years.*

Reactive: Adaptation that is undertaken in response to an effect of climate change that has already been experienced. *Example: Individual houses that are upgraded to new building standards only after a cyclone destroys their roofs.*

Private adaptation—private benefit: Adaptation taken by a person or business that benefits only that particular individual or business. *Example: Installing a water tank to ensure water availability during a dry spell.*

Private adaptation—public benefit: Adaptation taken by a person or business that is of benefit both to that person or business but also to the public more broadly. *Example: Farmer taking action to reduce fertilizer-laden runoff and erosion of topsoil during intense rainfall events, thus maintaining the viability of his farm whilst reducing the impact on the environment (e.g. coral reef).*

Public adaptation: Adaptation undertaken by a public entity to benefit the broader community. *Example: A local government undertakes beach nourishment activities to ensure that the beach is available to the public for recreation despite sea-level rise. Example: A surf life saving club relocates to a higher position after being frequently inundated by water during high tides.*

Timing of Adaptation in the Context of Uncertainty

There are uncertainties around our knowledge of future climate change, especially at the local scales relevant to adaptation policymakers and planners. Although these uncertainties are relatively small for temperature-related events, such as heat waves and sea-level rise, there are greater uncertainties associated with estimates of how rainfall and windstorm will change in the future. In consequence, anticipatory or proactive adaptation runs the risk that the action taken turns out to be inappropriate for the climate change that actually happens. Early action may create *lock-in* to a determined future pathway, which may be impossible to undo without prohibitive expense and effort, for example, expensive infrastructure that take many years to plan and build, such as flood protection works. This is termed *path dependency*.

One way to minimise this risk is to undertake *no-regrets* or *low-regrets* actions that deliver benefits across a wide range of potential climate futures and/or deliver benefits under present-day climate conditions as well as in the future. One example concerns people who live in flood-prone suburbs. They may take action to reduce their exposure to floods, for example by raising floor levels. This may prepare them for the effects of future climate change if flooding occurs more frequently.

Climate change unfolds over time with different impacts occurring at different rates. Therefore, we can avoid path dependency and lock-in by taking a *pathways approach* to adaptation. This involves mapping out the various adaptation options, and deciding where and when the climate change trigger points lie, which will require a decision to be made about whether or not to undertake a particular option.

Adaptation or Maladaptation?

A maladaptation is defined by the IPCC (2014) as "an action that may lead to increased risk of adverse climate-related outcomes, increased vulnerability to climate change, or diminished welfare, now or in the future." Maladaptation results in unintended negative consequences. It may occur for a number of reasons. First, an adaptation may addresses one sector but fail to account for negative flow-on effects in other sectors or to other people's values (e.g. a sea wall may protect someone's house but result in the loss of the beach and its amenity values to the community). Second, an adaptation may produce good results in the short term but fail in the longer term—a risk that may accompany many low-regrets actions. For example, a flood mitigation dam built to protect to flood levels anticipated over the next 30 years may fail on longer timescales even though its planned operational lifespan is 60-70 years. An adaptation plan needs to assess each action being considered against its potential for maladaptation.

Some Examples of Actual or Potential Maladaptive Actions

- Failure to anticipate future climates. Large engineering projects that are inadequate for future climates. Intensive use of non-renewable resources (e.g. groundwater) to solve immediate adaptation problem
- Engineered defenses that preclude alternative approaches such as ecosystem-based adaptation
- Adaptation actions not taking wider impacts into account
- Awaiting more information, or not doing so, and eventually acting either too early or too late. Awaiting better projections rather than using scenario planning and adaptive management approaches
- Forgoing longer term benefits in favor of immediate adaptive actions; depletion of natural capital leading to greater vulnerability
- Locking into a path dependence, making path correction difficult and often too late
- Unavoidable ex post maladaptation, e.g., expanding irrigation that eventually will have to be replaced in the distant future
- Moral hazard, such as encouraging inappropriate risk-taking based, e.g. on insurance or social security net

- Adopting actions that ignore local relationships, traditions, traditional knowledge, or property rights, leading to eventual failure
- Adopting actions that favour directly or indirectly one group over others leading to breakdown and possibly conflict
- Retaining traditional responses that are no longer appropriate
- Migration may be adaptive or maladaptive or both depending on context and the individuals involved.

Limits and Barriers to Adaptation

Adaptation is not a magic bullet—climate change may happen so quickly, or be so severe, that adaptation becomes impossible—either there are no strategies to address the risk, or they become too expensive, or the consequences of the adaptation are considered unacceptable. In this case, the climate change has reached a threshold or limit to adaptation. Limits may be ecological, physical, economic, technological or societal.

An example of an economic limit is where the cost of protecting an asset against sea-level rise by building a sea wall may be acceptable where the level of protection meets the risk over the next few decades, but the cost to meet the risk at the end of the century far exceeds the value of the asset being protected, making the expenditure impossible to justify.

Coral bleaching is an ecological limit. Corals, especially when in good health, can survive a modest amount of warming. But when ocean waters warm by just a few degrees above the long-term average, coral bleaching occurs. A few warm episodes, and there is widespread coral mortality.

[...]

A barrier to adaptation has been defined as "an obstacle that can be overcome with concerted effort" (Moser and Ekstrom 2010). In fact, the distinction between a limit and a barrier is a fine one, and not always of practical significance. Community opposition to attempts by local councils to zone land at risk of future flooding as unsuitable for development may strictly be described as a barrier, although some councils where the communities are particularly intransigent might term it a limit!

Linking Adaptation and Mitigation: Realising Co-Benefits

Adaptation should not be undertaken in isolation, but with an eye to any *co-benefits* for mitigation, sustainability and, in developing countries, development. Co-benefits are "the positive effects that a policy or measure aimed at one objective might have on other objectives" (IPCC 2014).

An example of adaptation with co-benefits for mitigation is the move towards "blue-green" cities. These bring together water management and green infrastructure to create more natural urban environments that are adaptive and resilient to climate change, while at the same time sequestering carbon and reducing energy demand.

CHAPTER 3

Is Future Environmental Catastrophe Avoidable?

Climate Change Will Impact the Environment in Numerous Ways

Union of Concerned Scientists

The Union of Concerned Scientists is a nonprofit advocacy group representing scientists and public citizens concerned about science-related issues.

G lobal warming is already having significant and costly effects on our communities, our health, and our climate.

Unless we take immediate action to reduce global warming emissions, these impacts will continue to intensify, grow ever more costly and damaging, and increasingly affect the entire planet— including you, your community, and your family.

Rising Seas and Increased Coastal Flooding

Average global sea level has increased eight inches since 1880, but is rising much faster on the US East Coast and Gulf of Mexico. Global warming is now accelerating the rate of sea level rise, increasing flooding risks to low-lying communities and high-risk coastal properties whose development has been encouraged by today's flood insurance system.

Longer and More Damaging Wildfire Seasons

Wildfires are increasing and wildfire season is getting longer in the Western US as temperatures rise. Higher spring and summer temperatures and earlier spring snow-melt result in forests that are hotter and drier for longer periods of time, priming conditions for wildfires to ignite and spread.

"Global Warming Impacts," Union of Concerned Scientists. Reprinted by permission.

More Destructive Hurricanes

While hurricanes are a natural part of our climate system, recent research indicates that their destructive power, or intensity, has been growing since the 1970s, particularly in the North Atlantic region.

More Frequent and Intense Heat Waves

Dangerously hot weather is already occurring more frequently than it did 60 years ago—and scientists expect heat waves to become more frequent and severe as global warming intensifies. This increase in heat waves creates serious health risks, and can lead to heat exhaustion, heat stroke, and aggravate existing medical conditions.

Military Bases at Risk

Rising seas will increasingly flood many of our coastal military bases.

National Landmarks at Risk

The growing consequences of climate change are putting many of the country's most iconic and historic sites at risk, from Ellis Island to the Everglades, Cape Canaveral to California's César Chávez National Monument.

Costly and Growing Health Impacts

Climate change has significant implications for our health. Rising temperatures will likely lead to increased air pollution, a longer and more intense allergy season, the spread of insect-borne diseases, more frequent and dangerous heat waves, and heavier rainstorms and flooding. All of these changes pose serious, and costly, risks to public health.

An Increase in Extreme Weather Events

Strong scientific evidence shows that global warming is increasing certain types of extreme weather events, including heat waves, coastal flooding, extreme precipitation events, and more severe droughts. Global warming also creates conditions that can lead to more powerful hurricanes.

Heavier Precipitation and Flooding

As temperatures increase, more rain falls during the heaviest downpours, increasing the risk of flooding events. Very heavy precipitation events, defined as the heaviest one percent of storms, now drop 67 percent more precipitation in the Northeast, 31 percent more in the Midwest and 15 percent more in the Great Plains than they did 50 years ago.

Destruction of Marine Ecosystems

Higher concentrations of CO_2 in the atmosphere, due to the burning of fossil fuels, is making oceans both warmer and more acidic. These two effects threaten the survival of marine life. Corals, shellfish, and phytoplankton, which are the base of the food chain, are particularly at risk.

More Severe Droughts in Some Areas

Climate change affects a variety of factors associated with drought and is likely to increase drought risk in certain regions. As temperatures have warmed, the prevalence and duration of drought has increased in the western US and climate models unanimously project increased drought in the American Southwest.

Widespread Forest Death in the Rocky Mountains

Tens of millions of trees have died in the Rocky Mountains over the past 15 years, victims of a climate-driven triple assault of tree-killing insects, wildfires, and stress from heat and drought.

Increased Pressure on Groundwater Supplies

As the climate changes in response to global warming, longer and more severe droughts are projected for the western US. The resulting dry conditions will increase the pressure on groundwater supplies as more is pumped to meet demand even as less precipitation falls to replenish it. In California, water and wastewater utilities have an opportunity to significantly increase clean energy in the state's water sector.

Growing Risks to Our Electricity Supply

Our aging electricity infrastructure is increasingly vulnerable to the growing consequences of global warming, including sea level rise, extreme heat, heightened wildfire risk, and drought and other water supply issues.

Changing Seasons

Spring arrives much earlier than it used to—10 days earlier on average in the northern hemisphere. Snow melts earlier. Reservoirs fill too early and water needs to be released for flood control. Vegetation and soils dry out earlier, setting the stage for longer and more damaging wildfire seasons.

Melting Ice

Temperatures are rising in the planet's polar regions, especially in the Arctic, and the vast majority of the world's glaciers are melting faster than new snow and ice can replenish them. Scientists expect the rate of melting to accelerate, with serious implications for future sea level rise.

Disruptions to Food Supplies

Rising temperatures and the accompanying impacts of global warming—including more frequent heat waves, heavier precipitation in some regions, and more severe droughts in others —has significant implications for crop and meat production. Global warming has the potential to seriously disrupt our food supply, drive costs upward, and affect everything from coffee to cattle, from staple food crops to the garden in your backyard.

Plant and Animal Range Shifts

A changing climate affects the range of plants and animals, changing their behavior and causing disruptions up and down the food chain. The range of some warm-weather species will expand, while those that depend on cooler environments will face shrinking habitats and potential extinction.

The Potential for Abrupt Climate Change

Scientists know that Earth's climate has changed abruptly in the past. Even though it is unlikely to occur in the near future, global warming may increase the risk of such events. One of the most significant potential mechanisms is a shift in an ocean circulation pattern known as thermohaline circulation, which would have widespread consequences for Europe and the US East Coast.

Adapting to a Changing Climate Is a Challenge, but Also an Opportunity for Progress

Saleemul Huq

Saleemul Huq is director of the International Centre for Climate Change & Development and a senior fellow in the Climate Change Group at the International Institute for Environment and Development.

Humanity has been adapting to all kinds of conditions, especially climatic conditions, for millennia and has done so with relative success so far. Human societies will continue to do so in response to potential adverse impacts of climate change as well. However, the level of such adverse impacts can be reduced considerably by pro-active or planned adaptation. The issue being addressed here is to what extent we can learn from the past and the science about the future to plan in advance to reduce those adverse impacts when they occur.

Questions being responded to:

1. Is the way we currently plan for the future and react to unexpected change sufficient to accommodate the uncertainty, scale, long lead time, and complexity associated with climate impacts?

2. For example, are current decision-making processes used by governments able to incorporate the long-term nature, surprises, heightened change and variability and the uncertainty of climate change or does such decision making require an entirely new approach?

3. If so, what needs to change? And why?

"Adapting to Climate Change: A Challenge and Opportunity," by Saleemul Huq, World Resource Institute. Reprinted by permission.

4. If not, how should current practices be harnessed to plan for and react to climate risks today and in the future?

I will argue that dealing with (or adapting to) the adverse impacts of human induced climate change is something that our generation and the next will have to learn to do in all countries, but starting in the poorest and most vulnerable countries (and the poorest and most vulnerable communities in all countries) for decades to come. If efforts to reduce global emissions of greenhouse gases fail to keep mean global temperature increase below 3 or 3.5 degrees Centigrade (the current trajectory) then such adverse impacts are likely to be of a globally catastrophic magnitude and may be beyond adaptation in many countries and communities.

However, even if global temperature rise is kept to below 2 degrees Centigrade (the current level of aspiration) many ecosystems and communities (perhaps involving hundreds of millions of mostly poor and vulnerable people) face severe adverse impacts. Such adverse impacts will occur first (and indeed may already be occurring) in the most vulnerable regions of the world where the poor make up the largest part of the population, but will in time also affect many richer parts of the world.

Thus, while over time all nations will have to learn to adapt to the adverse impacts of climate change, the poorest countries are the ones that will have to do so first (and indeed are already doing so). However, our knowledge and experience of what to expect and then how to prepare for it, is still in its infancy and we will collectively have to climb a very steep learning curve.

In answering the above set of questions I will argue that:

1. We are currently not well placed to deal with these kinds of long-term problems, either at the global or national levels (although countries do differ from one another in this respect).

2. Current decision-making processes, at both global as well as national level, are inadequate but responding to climate change presents an opportunity to do things differently.

3. What needs to change is the way decisions are made and implemented.

4. Present processes, structures and institutions, even if inadequate, cannot be wished away and must be involved in the change.

5. In developing a new paradigm of learning and decision-making on adaptation to climate change, the rich (countries and people) can learn from the poor (countries and communities).

Adaptation to Climate Variability vs. Adaptation to Climate Change?

It can be argued that mankind has been adapting to all kinds of conditions, especially climatic conditions, for millennia and has done so with relative success so far. This is indeed true and human societies will continue to do so in response to potential adverse impacts of climate change as well. However, the level of such adverse impacts can be reduced considerably by pro-active or planned adaptation. The issue being addressed here is to what extent can we learn from the past and the science about the future to plan in advance to reduce those adverse impacts when they occur (acknowledging that adaptation cannot reduce adverse impacts to zero)?

There are generally two types of potential future impacts of climate change that are considered to require action (while acknowledging that there are also likely to be some benefits from climate change in some places for some communities, I am going to deal with the adverse impacts only). These are *climatic hazards* such as floods, droughts and hurricanes which are likely to become more frequent or more severe (or both) and *slow-onset hazards* such as increasing salinity in low lying coasts and eventual inundation due to sea level rise.

Dealing with the first kind of climate hazards is not new, either at national or global level. Floods, droughts and hurricanes are well known phenomena which affect many parts of the world. However, preparing for the increased frequency and/or increased magnitude of events is something we have only just started to think about (both at the global as well as national level). One example is the way that the global disaster management community is geared to respond to events after they occur (e.g. the Tsunami in the Indian Ocean or the more recent earthquake in Haiti) but are not at all well prepared in advance of the events. The paradigm shift that is needed is to move away from the current reactive mode to a more pro-active mode or from disaster management (post disaster) to disaster preparedness (or disaster risk reduction). Such problems also occur at national level with Hurricane Katrina in the United States providing a stark example of the richest and most technologically advanced country in the world failing to protect the lives of some of its poorest and most vulnerable citizens in the ninth Ward of New Orleans.

On the other hand some of the poorest and most vulnerable countries have shown that taking pro-active measures can indeed reduce adverse impacts significantly. I will give one example from Bangladesh which was hit by a devastating cyclone in 1991 which killed over 100,000 people. Nearly two decades later in 2007 Cyclone Sidr, of similar magnitude, hit the country and only 3,000 or so people died (mostly fishermen on boats who could not get back to land) with over 2 million people successfully evacuated to cyclone shelters. This can be attributed largely to an extensive programme of building cyclone shelters around the entire coast, combined with developing strong early warning systems (including both the technical aspects of weather tracking and public outreach using Red Crescent and NGO volunteers as well as education in schools, etc) in the last decade. In contrast, another cyclone (Cyclone Nargis) that hit the neighbouring country of Myanmar (formerly Burma) a few months later, killed over 140,000 people—mainly due to the lack of any kind of preparation by the government. It should be noted that although the loss of human lives was reduced in Bangladesh from Cyclone Sidr, there was nevertheless a great deal of loss to infrastructure and the economy (so losses were not reduced to zero) and that the measures that were taken were not done for climate change reasons.

Thus, adapting to well known climatic hazards such as cyclones, droughts and floods are a good place to start to include adaptation to climate change but the two are not the same. Adaptation to climate change (ACC) includes longer-term, possibly slow-onset hazards which are not always included in run-of-the mill disaster management, or what might be termed adaptation to climate variability (ACV).

Adaptation *in situ* vs. Planned Re-Location (or Assisted Migration)

For the early years of adaptation studies it was assumed that adaptation to climate change was about assisting communities to continue (as best they could) to live their lives and earn their livelihoods without having to move. This might be termed adaptation *in situ*. It was thus assumed that adaptation to climate change (unlike mitigation) was a local (or national) phenomenon, and not a global (or cross-border) one. However, this is clearly no longer true as some parts of the world (such as some low lying coasts of islands and deltas, drylands in mid-continents and some highlands) are no longer able to sustain the communities currently living there. These communities will have to be helped to move somewhere else (whether within their own national borders or across international borders if their country itself disappears). While it can be argued that migration has been an age-old human response either to adversity or seeking new opportunities, the climate change-induced need to re-locate is something new in that it is a global responsibility to help those affected communities to re-locate in a planned and assisted manner (otherwise they will migrate anyway in an unplanned manner).

This will require new ways of dealing with migrants (or refugees) both internationally across borders as well within countries, for which we are not well prepared.

Adaptation to Climate Change vs. Development

It has been argued by some that adaptation to climate change is just the same as development (or even sustainable development, or more recently climate-resilient development). While such a case can indeed be made, I will argue that adaptation to climate change will require some new attributes that have not (so far) been associated with traditional development. The first is the need to be science-oriented. Climate change impacts are still only vaguely known within the scientific community and our knowledge of such impacts (at the global as well as national level) will need to grow rapidly over time. Decision-makers (whether global or national) will need to be hooked-up with their respective scientific communities in order to be aware of the latest developments in climate science.

Another attribute will be the need to build awareness and capacity on climate change amongst different stakeholders from within as well as outside governments. Indeed the entire next generation of school children and university graduates will need to have some level of climate literacy.

Bottom-Up vs. Top-Down (Globally and Nationally)

Until recently adaptation to climate change has been seen largely as a global issue, emanating from the scientific community (such as the IPCC) and global policy-making (such as the UNFCCC). However, more recently some governments have started to take action at a national level. At the same time many actors working at community level are also taking action. It is interesting to note that such actions are taking place first in the poorest countries and communities. Thus, for example, the first countries to produce their National Adaptation Plans of Action (NAPAs) were the forty-eight least developed countries (LDCs).

These were carried out in a quick-and-dirty manner to use existing scientific information on potential impacts of climate change within those countries, develop adaptation actions through a participatory manner and prioritise those actions. Some of the countries have moved on to implementing some of the adaptation actions identified in their respective NAPAs. While far from perfect as scientific and technical exercises, the NAPAs enabled the LDCs to develop their knowledge and capacities on climate change and work out the inter-institutional aspects of decision-making, which are mostly the same in all countries, whether rich or poor.

Thus now that the richer countries are beginning to develop their own adaptation plans, and are able to bring much greater amounts of financial and intellectual resources to bear, nevertheless they could learn much from the efforts of the poorest countries as many of the institutional problems are the same.

In a similar vein many actors working with some of the poorest and most vulnerable communities in the developing world have also been developing actions (now called Community Based Adaptation or CBA) and have been sharing their experiences and learning through a series of international conferences on CBA held over the last few years.

Again many decision-makers at national and global level can learn much from these actors working at the grass-roots on how to inform and empower people to make their own decisions about their own futures.

Conclusions

The last few examples cited above enable us to think of a new paradigm of learning and decision-making on adaptation to climate change at global as well as national levels, where the rich (countries and people) can learn from the poor (both countries as well as communities).

Addressing Environmental Concerns Can Stimulate Growth in Industries Around the World

European Environment Agency

The European Environment Agency (EEA) is the EU's agency dedicated to studying and understanding climate change and environmental threats.

D ecades of intensive use of stocks of natural capital and ecosystem degradation by developed countries to fuel economic development have resulted in global warming, loss of biodiversity and various negative impacts on our health. Even though many of the immediate impacts lie outside Europe's direct influence, they have significant consequences and will create potential risks for the resilience and sustainable development of the European economy and society.

Emerging and developing economies have in recent years replicated this trend but at a much faster speed driven by increasing populations, growing numbers of middle class consumers, and rapidly changing consumption patterns towards levels in developed countries; unprecedented financial flows chasing scarcer energy and raw materials; unparalleled shifts in economic power, growth, and trade patterns from advanced to emerging and developing economies; and, delocalisation of production driven by price competition.

Climate change is one of the most obvious effects of these past developments: breaching the 2°C target is probably the most tangible example of the risk of going beyond planetary boundaries. The long-term ambition of achieving 80 to 95% reductions in CO_2 emissions by 2050 in Europe to stay in line with the above

"Future Environmental Priorities: Some Reflections," European Environment Agency (EEA), March 6, 2016. https://www.eea.europa.eu/soer/synthesis/synthesis/chapter8 .xhtml. Licensed under CC BY 2.5 DK.

target, strongly argues for a fundamental transformation of Europe's current economy, with low-carbon energy and transport systems as central planks of the new economy—but not the only ones.

As in the past, future climate change impacts are expected to affect disproportionately the most vulnerable in society: children, the elderly, and the poor. On the positive side, greater access to green spaces, biodiversity, clean water and air benefit people's health. However, this too raises the question about the sharing of access and benefits, since often spatial planning and investment decisions favour the rich at the expense of the poor.

Well-maintained ecosystems and ecosystem services are essential to support climate change mitigation and adaptation objectives, and preserving biodiversity is a prerequisite for ensuring this. Balancing the role that ecosystems can play as a buffer against expected impacts with possible increased demands for new settlements on water and land, brings new challenges, for example, to spatial planners, architects and conservationists.

The ongoing race for substitution from carbon-intensive to low-carbon energy and materials is expected to further intensify demands on the terrestrial, aquatic and marine ecosystems and services (first and second generation biofuels provide an example here). As these demands increase, for example for chemical substitutes, there are likely to be increasing conflicts with existing uses for food, transport and leisure.

Many of the environmental challenges assessed in this report have been highlighted in previous EEA reports. What is different today is the speed at which interconnectedness spreads risks and increases uncertainties across the world. Sudden breakdowns in one area or geographical region can transmit large-scale failures through a whole network of economies, via contagion, feedbacks and other amplifications. The recent global financial crash or the Icelandic volcano episodes have demonstrated this.

Crises such as these have also shown how difficult it is for society to deal with risks. Well signposted and numerous early warnings are often widely ignored. At the same time, recent times offer many experiences, both good and bad, from which we can learn and so respond more quickly and more systematically to the challenges we face (for example, through multiple crisis management, climate negotiations, eco-innovations, information technologies, or global knowledge developments).

Against this back-drop, this final chapter reflects on some emerging future environmental priorities:

- Better implementation and further strengthening of current environmental priorities in climate change; nature and biodiversity; natural resource use and waste; environment, health and quality of life. Whilst these remain important priorities, managing the links between them will be paramount. Improving monitoring and enforcement of sectoral and environmental policies will ensure that environmental outcomes are achieved, give regulatory stability and support more effective governance.
- Dedicated management of natural capital and ecosystem services. Increasing resource efficiency and resilience emerge as key integrating concepts for dealing with environmental priorities, and for the many sectoral interests that depend on them.
- Coherent integration of environmental considerations across the many sectoral policy domains can help increase the efficiency with which natural resources are used and thus help greening the economy by reducing common pressures on the environment that originate from multiple sources and economic activities. Coherence will also lead to broad measures of progress rather than just against individual targets.
- Transformation to a green economy that addresses the long-term viability of natural capital within Europe and reduced dependency on it outside Europe.

The ongoing study on The Economics of Ecosystems and Biodiversity (TEEB) aligns with these ideas from the perspective of biodiversity and the ways in which investment in natural capital can be encouraged. Recommendations to policymakers include broad actions such as investing in green infrastructure to increase resilience, introducing payments for ecosystem services, removing harmful subsidies, establishing new regimes for natural capital accounting and cost-benefit analysis, and initiating specific actions to address the degradation of forests, coral reefs and fisheries as well as the links between ecosystem degradation and poverty.

Natural capital and ecosystem services provide an integral starting point for managing many of these interconnected issues, the systemic risks inherent in them, and the transformation to a new, greener, more resource efficient economy. There is no single "quick fix" for the challenges that Europe faces. Rather, as this report shows, there is a clear case for long-term, interconnected approaches to deal with them.

What this report also provides is evidence that existing European environmental policies present a robust basis on which to build new approaches that balance economic, social and environmental considerations. Future actions can draw on a set of key principles that have been established at European level: the integration of environmental considerations into other measures; precaution and prevention; rectification of damage at source; and the polluter-pays principle.

[...]

Stimulating Fundamental Transition Towards a Greener Economy in Europe

Greening the European economy can help further reduce environmental pressures and impacts. However, more fundamental conditions and actions that enable the transition to a truly "green economy," centred on natural capital and ecosystem services, will be needed to stay within planetary limits.

The need for a green economy also becomes stronger in this time of financial and economic crisis. Intuitively, a slumping economy might be considered positive for the environment: income drops or grows only slowly, accessing credit that allows overspending is more difficult and hence we produce and consume less, with a reduced burden on the environment. However, stagnant economies are often not able to make the necessary investments to secure a responsible environmental management, and see less innovation and less attention to environmental policy. Instead, when the economy returns to its previous growth path (as it usually does), it also tends to return to its previous pattern of eroding natural capital.

Thus, a green economy will require dedicated policy approaches embedded in a coherent, integrated strategy covering demand and supply aspects, both economy-wide and at the sectoral level. In this context, the key environmental principles of precaution, prevention, rectification of damage at source, and polluter pays, combined with a strong evidence base, remain most relevant and need to be more broadly and consistently applied.

The precautionary and prevention principles were inserted in the EU Treaty in order to help cope with the dynamics of complex natural systems. Their broader application during the transition to a green economy will steer innovations that break away from the often monopolistic and conventional technologies that have been shown to cause long-term harm to people and ecosystems.

The rectification of damage at source can be maximised through deeper integration across sectors and further advance the multiple gains from investments in green technologies. For example, investment in energy efficiency and renewable energies delivers benefits to the environment, employment, energy security, energy costs, and can help combat fuel poverty.

The polluter pays principle can stimulate a greening of the economy through taxes that allow market prices to reflect full costs of production, consumption and wastes. This can be achieved via greater use of fiscal reform which in addition to removing harmful subsidies, replaces distortionary taxes on economic "goods" such as labour and capital, with more efficient taxes on economic "bads," such as pollution and inefficient resource use.

In a broader perspective, "prices" as a facilitator of trade-offs can help improve further progress in sectoral integration and resource efficiency but more fundamentally shift behaviours across governments, businesses and citizens in Europe and globally. However, for this to happen—as known for decades, but rarely applied—prices need to reflect the true economic, environmental and social value of resources, relative to available substitutes.

Evidence of the benefits of fiscal reform has grown in recent years. Such benefits include environmental improvements, employment gains, a stimulus to eco-innovation and more efficient tax systems. Studies show the benefits from modest environmental tax reform in several European countries that have been implemented over the last 20 years. Similarly, they convincingly demonstrate the advantages of additional reforms designed to achieve the EU climate and resource efficiency goals.

The revenues from environmental taxes vary significantly across EU Member States, from more than 5% of GDP in Denmark to less than 2% in Spain, Lithuania, Romania, and Latvia in 2008. Despite the large benefits of such taxes, and consistent policy support over the last 20 years from OECD and the EU, environmental tax revenues as a proportion of overall tax revenues in the EU are at their lowest level in more than a decade, even if the number of environmental taxes is increasing.

There is substantial potential for fiscal reform in support of the triple objectives of greening the economy, supporting deficit reduction policies in many EU Member States and responding to ageing populations. These range from removing harmful subsidies and exemptions on fossil fuels, fisheries and agriculture, to establishing taxes and extending permits on the consumption of the critical natural capital that underpins a green economy (such as carbon, water and land).

A further component of a green economy transition is to move to accounting fully for natural capital—and to thus go beyond GDP as a measure of economic growth. Doing so will enable societies to record the full price of our way of life, reveal concealed debts being forwarded to future generations, make explicit ancillary benefits, highlight new ways for economic development and jobs in a green economy based on green infrastructure, and reframe the base for fiscal revenues and their use.

In practical terms, looking "Beyond GDP" means creating measures that convey not just what we have produced in the last year but also the state of the natural capital that determines what we can produce sustainably now and in the future. Specifically, these measures would comprise two additional items, beyond the depreciation of our man-made, physical capital: the depletion of our non-renewable natural resources and how much income they generate; and the degradation of our ecosystem capital and how we should reinvest to maintain the current capacity of using ecosystem services.

A genuine measurement of natural capital depreciation should take account of the many functions of natural ecosystems to ensure that management of one function does not result in the degradation of other functions. In the case of ecosystems, the management objective is not to maintain a flow of income but to maintain the ecosystem capacity of delivering the full bundle of services. Therefore a key element of any valuation of ecosystem degradation needs to be an appraisal of required restoration costs. This can be done, for example through estimates of the reduction of yields, replantation, pollution abatement, and green infrastructures restoration. The methodology for this approach is already being tested for Europe.

Accounting fully for natural capital will also require new classifications, ideally linked to existing ones as described in the statistical frameworks and system of national accounts (SNA). Important examples are emerging, for example in the area of ecosystem services or carbon accounting and carbon crediting.

In addition, a new information environment will have to address the widespread lack of accountability and transparency, and the loss of trust amongst citizens in governments, science and business. The challenge now is to improve the knowledge base in order to support more accountable and participatory decision making. Providing access to information is essential for effective governance; but engaging people in collecting data and sharing their lay knowledge is arguably just as important.

A further reflection concerns equipping Europeans with the skills to make the transformation to a green economy. Education, research and industrial policy have roles to play here by providing the next generation of materials, technologies, processes and indicators (for example related to systemic risks and vulnerabilities) that help reduce Europe's dependencies, increase resource efficiencies and enhance economic competitiveness in line with the EU2020 strategy.

Other factors include incentives for businesses using new financial mechanisms, retraining existing workers to contribute to green industries, and deploying unskilled workers displaced by delocalised production. A good example is the European recycling industry which holds a 50% global market and has been increasing employment by some 10% annually, mostly for unskilled workers.

More generally, many multi-national businesses are also responding to the natural capital challenge, recognising that the future economy must have the means to manage, value and trade such capital. There is scope to foster further the role of small and medium enterprises in natural capital management.

In addition, new forms of governance will also be needed to better reflect this shared dependence on natural capital. Over recent decades the role played by civil society institutions—such as banks, insurance companies, multi-national companies, non-governmental organisations, and global institutions such as the World Trade Organisation—has increased compared to the power of territorially bounded nation states. Balancing interests will be essential to manage shared interests and dependencies around natural capital. On the eve of the 20-year anniversary of the UN

Commission for Sustainable Development in 2012, the slogan think global, act local seems more appropriate than ever.

The responses to recent systemic shocks highlights society's predilection for short-term crisis management over long-term decision-making and actions while at the same time showing the benefits of coherent, albeit short-term, global responses in dealing with such risks. The experience should not be a surprise given the strong bias towards governance that deals with short-term considerations aligned to the policy cycle (4 to 7 years) at the expense of long-term challenges, although there are examples in several EU Member States of structures being established to consider long-term challenges.

The transformation towards a greener European economy will help secure the long-term sustainability of Europe and its neighbourhood, but it will also require shifts in attitudes. Examples include encouraging wider participation by Europeans in the management of natural capital and ecosystem services, creation of new and innovative solutions to use resources efficiently, introduction of fiscal reforms, and involvement of citizens through education and different forms of social media in tackling global issues such as meeting the 2°C climate target. The seeds for future actions exist: the task ahead is to help them take root and flourish.

Mitigating Climate Change Would Require Unprecedented Action

Intergovernmental Panel on Climate Change

The Intergovernmental Panel on Climate Change (IPCC) is a UN body made up of experts from around the world that provides reports on climate change.

C ontinued emission of greenhouse gases will cause further warming and long-lasting changes in all components of the climate system, increasing the likelihood of severe, pervasive and irreversible impacts for people and ecosystems. Limiting climate change would require substantial and sustained reductions in greenhouse gas emissions which, together with adaptation, can limit climate change risks.

[...]

Projected Changes in the Climate System

Surface temperature is projected to rise over the 21st century under all assessed emission scenarios. It is *very likely* that heat waves will occur more often and last longer, and that extreme precipitation events will become more intense and frequent in many regions. The ocean will continue to warm and acidify, and global mean sea level to rise.

Future climate will depend on committed warming caused by past anthropogenic emissions, as well as future anthropogenic emissions and natural climate variability. The global mean surface temperature change for the period 2016–2035 relative to 1986–2005 is similar for the four RCPs [Representative Concentration Pathways] and will *likely* be in the range 0.3°C to 0.7°C (*medium*

"Climate Change 2014 Synthesis Report Summary for Policymakers," Intergovernmental Panel on Climate Change (IPCC). Reprinted by permission.

confidence). This assumes that there will be no major volcanic eruptions or changes in some natural sources (e.g., CH_4 and N_2O), or unexpected changes in total solar irradiance. By mid-21st century, the magnitude of the projected climate change is substantially affected by the choice of emissions scenario.

[...]

It is *virtually certain* that there will be more frequent hot and fewer cold temperature extremes over most land areas on daily and seasonal timescales, as global mean surface temperature increases. It is *very likely* that heat waves will occur with a higher frequency and longer duration. Occasional cold winter extremes will continue to occur.

Changes in precipitation will not be uniform. The high latitudes and the equatorial Pacific are *likely* to experience an increase in annual mean precipitation under the RCP8.5 scenario. In many mid-latitude and subtropical dry regions, mean precipitation will *likely* decrease, while in many mid-latitude wet regions, mean precipitation will *likely* increase under the RCP8.5 scenario. Extreme precipitation events over most of the mid-latitude land masses and over wet tropical regions will very *likely* become more intense and more frequent.

The global ocean will continue to warm during the 21st century, with the strongest warming projected for the surface in tropical and Northern Hemisphere subtropical regions.

[...]

Future Risks and Impacts Caused by a Changing Climate

Climate change will amplify existing risks and create new risks for natural and human systems. Risks are unevenly distributed and are generally greater for disadvantaged people and communities in countries at all levels of development.

Risk of climate-related impacts results from the interaction of climate-related hazards (including hazardous events and trends) with the vulnerability and exposure of human and natural systems, including their ability to adapt. Rising rates and magnitudes of warming and other changes in the climate system, accompanied by ocean acidification, increase the risk of severe, pervasive and in some cases irreversible detrimental impacts. Some risks are particularly relevant for individual regions, while others are global. The overall risks of future climate change impacts can be reduced by limiting the rate and magnitude of climate change, including ocean acidification. The precise levels of climate change sufficient to trigger abrupt and irreversible change remain uncertain, but the risk associated with crossing such thresholds increases with rising temperature (*medium confidence*). For risk assessment, it is important to evaluate the widest possible range of impacts, including low-probability outcomes with large consequences.

A large fraction of species faces increased extinction risk due to climate change during and beyond the 21st century, especially as climate change interacts with other stressors (*high confidence*). Most plant species cannot naturally shift their geographical ranges sufficiently fast to keep up with current and high projected rates of climate change in most landscapes; most small mammals and freshwater mollusks will not be able to keep up at the rates projected under RCP4.5 and above in at landscapes in this century (*high confidence*). Future risk is indicated to be high by the observation that natural global climate change at rates lower than current anthropogenic climate change caused significant ecosystem shifts and species extinctions during the past millions of years. Marine organisms will face progressively lower oxygen levels and high rates and magnitudes of ocean acidification (*high confidence*), with associated risks exacerbated by rising ocean temperature extremes (*medium confidence*). Coral reefs and polar ecosystems are highly vulnerable. Coastal systems and low-lying areas are at risk from sea level rise, which will continue for centuries even if the global mean temperature is stabilized (*high confidence*).

Climate change is projected to undermine food security. Due to projected climate change by the mid-21st century and beyond, global marine species redistribution and marine biodiversity reduction in sensitive regions will challenge the sustained provision of fisheries productivity and other ecosystem services (*high confidence*). For wheat, rice and maize in tropical and temperate regions, climate change without adaptation is projected to negatively impact production for local temperature increases of 2°C or more above late 20th century levels, although individual locations may benefit (*medium confidence*). Global temperature increases of ~4°C or more above late 20th century levels, combined with increasing food demand, would pose large risks to food security globally (*high confidence*). Climate change is projected to reduce renewable surface water and groundwater resources in most dry subtropical regions (*robust evidence, high agreement*), intensifying competition for water among sectors (*limited evidence, medium agreement*).

Until mid-century, projected climate change will impact human health mainly by exacerbating health problems that already exist (*very high confidence*). Throughout the 21st century, climate change is expected to lead to increases in ill-health in many regions and especially in developing countries with low income, as compared to a baseline without climate change (*high confidence*). By 2100 for RCP8.5, the combination of high temperature and humidity in some areas for parts of the year is expected to compromise common human activities, including growing food and working outdoors (*high confidence*).

In urban areas climate change is projected to increase risks for people, assets, economies and ecosystems, including risks from heat stress, storms and extreme precipitation, inland and coastal flooding, landslides, air pollution, drought, water scarcity, sea level rise and storm surges (*very high confidence*). These risks are amplified for those lacking essential infrastructure and services or living in exposed areas.

Rural areas are expected to experience major impacts on water availability and supply, food security, infrastructure and agricultural incomes, including shifts in the production areas of food and non-food crops around the world (*high confidence*).

Aggregate economic losses accelerate with increasing temperature (*limited evidence, high agreement*), but global economic impacts from climate change are currently difficult to estimate. From a poverty perspective, climate change impacts are projected to slow down economic growth, make poverty reduction more difficult, further erode food security and prolong existing and create new poverty traps, the latter particularly in urban areas and emerging hotspots of hunger (*medium confidence*). International dimensions such as trade and relations among states are also important for understanding the risks of climate change at regional scales.

Climate change is projected to increase displacement of people (*medium evidence, high agreement*). Populations that lack the resources for planned migration experience higher exposure to extreme weather events, particularly in developing countries with low income. Climate change can indirectly increase risks of violent conflicts by amplifying well-documented drivers of these conflicts such as poverty and economic shocks (*medium confidence*).

Climate Change Beyond 2100, Irreversibility and Abrupt Change

Many aspects of climate change and associated impacts will continue for centuries, even if anthropogenic emissions of greenhouse gases are stopped. The risks of abrupt or irreversible changes increase as the magnitude of the warming increases.

Warming will continue beyond 2100 under all RCP scenarios except RCP2.6. Surface temperatures will remain approximately constant at elevated levels for many centuries after a complete cessation of net anthropogenic CO_2 emissions. A large fraction of anthropogenic climate change resulting from CO_2 emissions is irreversible on a multi-century to millennial timescale, except in the case of a large net removal of CO_2 from the atmosphere over a sustained period.

Stabilization of global average surface temperature does not imply stabilization for all aspects of the climate system. Shifting biomes, soil carbon, ice sheets, ocean temperatures and associated sea level rise all have their own intrinsic long timescales which will result in changes lasting hundreds to thousands of years after global surface temperature is stabilized.

There is *high confidence* that ocean acidification will increase for centuries if CO_2 emissions continue, and will strongly affect marine ecosystems.

It is *virtually certain* that global mean sea level rise will continue for many centuries beyond 2100, with the amount of rise dependent on future emissions. The threshold for the loss of the Greenland ice sheet over a millennium or more, and an associated sea level rise of up to 7 m, is greater than about 1°C (*low confidence*) but less than about 4°C (*medium confidence*) of global warming with respect to pre-industrial temperatures. Abrupt and irreversible ice loss from the Antarctic ice sheet is possible, but current evidence and understanding is insufficient to make a quantitative assessment.

Magnitudes and rates of climate change associated with medium- to high-emission scenarios pose an increased risk of abrupt and irreversible regional-scale change in the composition, structure and function of marine, terrestrial and freshwater ecosystems, including wetlands (*medium confidence*). A reduction in permafrost extent is *virtually certain* with continued rise in global temperatures.

[…]

Technology Will Not Stop Climate Change on Its Own

Howard J. Herzog

Howard J. Herzog is an author and a senior research engineer in the MIT Energy Initiative.

In a much-anticipated report, the Intergovernmental Panel on Climate Change (IPCC) said the world will need to take dramatic and drastic steps to avoid the catastrophic effects of climate change.

Featured prominently in the report is a discussion of a range of techniques for removing carbon dioxide from the air, called Carbon Dioxide Removal (CDR) technologies or negative emissions technologies (NETs). The IPCC said the world would need to rely significantly on these techniques to avoid increasing Earth's temperatures above 1.5 degrees Celsius, or 2.7 degrees Fahrenheit, compared to pre-industrial levels.

Given that the level of greenhouse gases continues to rise and the world's efforts at lowering emissions are falling way short of targets climate scientists recommend, what contribution we can expect from NETs is becoming a critical question. Can they actually work at a big enough scale?

What Are Negative Emissions Technologies?

There is a wide range of opinion on how big an impact these techniques can have in addressing climate change. I became involved in the debate because two of the most prominent negative emissions technologies involve CO_2 capture and storage (CCS), a technology that I have been researching for almost 30 years.

Many NETs remove the CO_2 from the atmosphere biologically through photosynthesis—the simplest example being afforestation,

"Why We Can't Reverse Climate Change with 'Negative Emissions' Technologies," by Howard J. Herzog, The Conversation. October 9, 2018. https://theconversation.com/why-we-cant-reverse-climate-change-with-negative-emissions-technologies-103504. Licensed Under CC BY 3.0.

or planting more trees. Depending on the specific technique, the carbon removed from the atmosphere may end up in soils, vegetation, the ocean, deep geological formations, or even in rocks.

NETs vary on their cost, scale (how many tons they can potentially remove from the atmosphere), technological readiness, environmental impacts and effectiveness. Afforestation/reforestation is the only NET to have been deployed commercially though others have been tested at smaller scales. For example, there are a number of efforts to produce biochar, a charcoal made with plant matter that has a net negative carbon balance.

A recent academic paper discusses the "costs, potentials, and side-effects" of the various NETs. Afforestation/reforestation is one of the least expensive options, with a cost on the order of tens of dollars per ton of CO_2, but the scope for carbon removal is small compared to other NETs.

On the other extreme is direct air capture, which covers a range of engineered systems meant to remove CO_2 from the air. The costs of direct air capture, which has been tested at small scales, are on the order of hundreds of dollars or more per ton of CO_2, but is on the high end in terms of the potential amount of CO_2 that can be removed.

In a 2014 IPCC report, a technology called bio-energy with carbon capture and storage (BECCS) received the most attention. This entails burning plant matter, or biomass, for energy and then collecting the CO_2 emissions and pumping the gases underground. Its cost is high, but not excessive, in the range of US\$100-200 per ton of CO_2 removed.

The biggest constraint on the size of its deployment relates to the availability of "low-carbon" biomass. There are carbon emissions associated with the growing, harvesting, and transporting of biomass, as well as potential carbon emissions due to land-use changes—for example, if forests are cut down in favor of other forms of biomass. These emissions must all be kept to a minimum for biomass to be "low-carbon" and for the overall scheme to result in negative emissions. Potential "low-carbon" biomass includes switchgrass or loblolly pine, as opposed to say corn, which is currently turned into liquid fuels and acknowledged to have a high carbon footprint.

Some of the proposed NETs are highly speculative. For example, ocean fertilization is generally not considered a realistic option because its environmental impact on the ocean is probably unacceptable. Also, there are questions about how effective it would be in removing CO_2.

Academic Takes

A 2017 study at the University of Michigan did a literature review of NETs. One the one hand, they showed that the literature was very bullish on NETs. It concluded these techniques could capture the equivalent of 37 gigatons (billion tons) of CO_2 per year at a cost of below $70 per metric ton. For comparison, the world currently emits about 38 gigatons of CO_2 a year.

However, I think this result should be taken with a large grain of salt, as they rated only one NET as established (afforestation/reforestation), three others as demonstrated (BECCS, biochar and modified agricultural practices), and the rest as speculative. In other words, these technologies have potential, but they have yet to be proven effective.

Other studies have a much harsher view of NETs. A study in Nature Climate Change from 2015 states, "There is no NET (or combination of NETs) currently available that could be implemented to meet the <2°C target without significant impact on either land, energy, water, nutrient, albedo or cost, and so 'plan A' must be to immediately and aggressively reduce GHG emissions." In another study from 2016, researchers Kevin Anderson and Glen Peters concluded "Negative-emission technologies are not an insurance policy, but rather an unjust and high-stakes gamble. There is a real risk they will be unable to deliver on the scale of their promise."

The bottom line is that NETs must be shown to work on a gigaton scale, at an affordable cost, and without serious environmental impacts. That has not happened yet. As seen from above, there is a wide range of opinion on whether this will ever happen.

Safety Net?

A critical question is what role NETs can play, both from a policy and economic point of view, as we struggle to stabilize the mean global temperature at an acceptable level.

One potential role for NETs is as an offset. This means that the amount of CO_2 removed from the atmosphere generates credits that offset emissions elsewhere. Using negative emissions this way can be a powerful policy or economic lever.

For example, with airline travel the best approach to net zero emissions may be to let that industry continue to emit CO_2, but offset those emissions using credits from NETs. Essentially those negative emissions are a way to compensate for the emissions from flying, which is expected to rely on fossil fuels for many years.

About 25 percent of our current carbon emissions can be classified as hard to mitigate. This offset model makes economic sense when the cost of negative emissions is less than the cost to cut emissions from the source itself. So if we can produce negative emissions from say BECCS at about $150 per ton of CO_2, they can economically be used to offset emissions from aircraft that would cost several hundred dollars per ton CO_2 to mitigate by changing how planes are fueled.

The economics of using NETs to correct an "overshoot" are very different.

We as a society seem unwilling to undertake sufficient efforts to reduce carbon emissions today at costs of tens of dollars per ton CO_2 in order to keep enough CO_2 out of the atmosphere to meet stabilization targets of 1.5 or 2 degrees Celsius. However, correcting an "overshoot" means we expect future generations to clean up our mess by removing CO_2 from the atmosphere at costs of hundreds of dollars or more per ton CO_2, which is what the future deployment of NETs may cost.

This makes no sense, economic or otherwise. If we are unwilling to use the relatively cheap mitigation technologies to lower carbon emissions available today, such as improved efficiency, increased renewables, or switching from coal to natural gas, what makes anyone think that future generations will use NETs, which are much, much more expensive?

That's why I see the role of NETs as an offset being very sound, with some deployment already happening today and increased deployment expected in the future. By contrast, treating NETs as a way to compensate for breaking the carbon budget and overshooting stabilization targets is more hope than reality. The technical, economic and environmental barriers of NETs are very real. In formulating climate policy, I believe we cannot count on the future use of NETs to compensate for our failure to do enough mitigation today.

CHAPTER 4

Do Individual Choices Have a Role in Addressing Environmental Catastrophe?

What Motivates Individuals to Take Action Against Climate Change?

Catherine Jex

Catherine Jex is a science writer who specializes in Earth sciences and climate change.

A conversation on tackling climate change can become heated very quickly, especially if it challenges our core political beliefs.

Psychologists have now found that almost anyone can be motivated to take action against climate change, by appealing to the so-called co-benefits. These are the benefits that go hand in hand with tackling climate change, such as social, economic, and scientific development.

"Simply saying that we should tackle an environmental problem because it's important has not worked, because it's so linked to an individual's political agenda," says co-author Professor Lars-Olof Johansson, from the University of Gothenburg, Sweden.

"But we can influence peoples' motivations if we talk about the effect of so-called co-benefits, instead of focussing on the science or the importance of tackling the problem of climate change," he says.

They also found that reducing pollution was one of the least motivating co-benefits in many countries.

The research is published in the journal *Nature Climate Change*.

Appeal to What People Already Believe

Co-author Gró Einarsdóttir, a PhD student from the University of Gothenburg, describes how emphasising the co-benefits of tackling climate change can influence people's motivation to act.

"Co-benefits are basically when you take things that many people already care about and connect this with taking action on climate or other environmental issues. These could be economic or scientific

"This Is How We Motivate People to Tackle Climate Change," by Catherine Jex, ScienceNordic, October 6, 2015. Reprinted by permission.

development, or simply living in a more pleasant and caring society," says Einarsdóttir.

The new research suggests that by addressing these co-benefits, politicians and communicators can circumnavigate the often insurmountable hurdle of trying to change a person's worldview in order to motivate them to support environmentally friendly measures.

"It's much easier to address the things that many people already care about and link these things to environmental action, like creating jobs and the state of their local community, rather than trying to change their stance on particular environmental issues," says Einarsdóttir.

"Simply saying to someone 'you have to change' doesn't work. But saying that 'even if you don't believe in these measures to combat climate change, but by implementing them we can improve society' is a win-win," says Johansson.

Global Surveys Reveal Common Motivations

Johansson and Einarsdóttir were part of a team of international researchers, led by Queensland University of Technology, Australia. They sent out an e-survey to university students in 24 countries, covering all inhabited continents.

Another smaller group of people from 10 of these countries also took part in the survey. This group represented people from all walks of life—different ages and occupations—and allowed the researchers to check that their findings were not only applicable to students.

All participants were quizzed on whether or not they thought tackling climate change was important, and their opinions on a number of co-benefits that could motivate them to act.

Out of the 6,196 participants, they found that development co-benefits, which encompass both economic and scientific development, such as creating new jobs in new technology sectors, and benevolence co-benefits, where communities become more caring and moral, were particularly effective.

Crucially, these co-benefits motivated people in all countries regardless of whether or not they "believed" in man made climate change, and motivated people far more than the prospect of cutting pollution.

Accepting Policies to Tackle Climate Change

According to Johansson, the results can be used in many ways to improve the public acceptance of mitigating climate change.

"For a politician, it's important that people accept environmental policies. So addressing co-benefits is one way of increasing acceptance," he says.

This could be particularly effective in countries where public acceptance of the underlying science is low, or in developing countries where the economic costs of tackling climate change may not be high on the agenda, says Johansson.

There May Not Always Be a Case for Co-Benefits

Dr. Steffen Kallbekken, Research Director at the Center for International Climate and Environmental Research (CICERO) and Director of the Center for International Climate and Energy Policy (CICEP) in Oslo, Norway, says that communicating the co-benefits of climate action, as this study argues, appears to be a sound strategy.

"If cutting greenhouse gas emissions involves benefits such as new jobs at a local wind farm or cleaner air, people are more likely to support climate action. But one limitation of this approach is that not all climate policies have co-benefits," says Kallbekken.

He emphasises that there will be situations in which some businesses will close down and some jobs will be lost without necessarily being compensated by new jobs or cleaner air in that same community.

"It's possible to choose the climate actions that deliver the largest co-benefits, but we will still also need strategies for those situations where the co-benefits do not exist or are not large enough to sway public opinion."

"One strategy could be to soften the blow by helping people transition to new jobs through job training or government incentives to establish new jobs in affected areas," he says.

There Are Steps Individuals Can Take to Mitigate Their Impact on the Environment

David Suzuki Foundation

The David Suzuki Foundation is a Canadian nonprofit dedicated to environmentalism.

As the world warms, extreme weather events are becoming more frequent and intense, sea levels are rising, prolonged droughts are putting pressure on food crops, and many animal and plant species are being driven to extinction. It's hard to imagine what we as individuals can do to resolve a problem of this scale and severity.

The good news: We are not alone. People, communities, cities, businesses, schools, faith groups and other organizations are taking action. We're fighting like our lives depend on it—because they do.

Get Charged Up with Renewables

The global push for cleaner, healthier energy is on. With costs dropping every day, renewable energy is the best choice for the environment and the economy.

People throughout Canada are leading on renewables, making a difference in towns, cities and rural areas. You can, too!

Start by sending a message to Canada's federal party leaders to get charged up with renewables now.

Green Your Commute

In Canada, transportation accounts for 24 per cent of climate-polluting emissions, a close second to the oil and gas industry.

The many ways to reduce your transportation emissions will also make you healthier, happier and save you a few bucks. Whenever and wherever you can:

"Top 10 Things You Can Do About Climate Change," David Suzuki Foundation, July 3, 2018. Reprinted by permission.

- Take public transit.
- Ride a bike.
- Car-share.
- Switch to an electric or hybrid vehicle.
- Fly less (if you do fly, make sure you offset your emissions).

Use Energy Wisely—Save Money, Too!

On a per capita basis, Canada is one of the top energy consumers in the world! By getting more energy efficient, you'll pollute less and save money.

The small changes you make add up:

- Change to energy-efficient light bulbs.
- Unplug computers, TVs and other electronics when you're not using them.
- Wash clothes in cold or warm (not hot) water.
- Dryers are energy hogs, so hang dry when you can and use dryer balls when you can't.
- Install a programmable thermostat.
- Look for the Energy Star label when buying new appliances.
- Winterize your home to prevent heat from escaping.
- Get a home or workplace energy audit to identify where you can make the most energy-saving gains.

Eat for a Climate-Stable Planet

> *"Eat food. Not too much. Mostly plants."* —Michael Pollan

Here are four simple changes you can make to your diet to reduce its climate impact.

- Eat meat-free meals.
- Buy organic and local whenever possible.
- Don't waste food.
- Grow your own.

Get more info on how to eat for the climate and how eating less meat will reduce Earth's heat.

P.S. You can also help save the planet by eating insects!

Consume Less, Waste Less, Enjoy Life More

"We use too much, too much of it is toxic and we don't share it very well. But that's not the way things have to be. Together, we can build a society based on better not more, sharing not selfishness, community not division." —The Story of Stuff

Focusing on life's simple pleasures—spending time in nature, being with loved ones and/or making a difference to others—provides more purpose, belonging and happiness than buying and consuming. Sharing, making, fixing, upcycling, repurposing and composting are all good places to start.

Divest from Fossil Fuels

Let industry know you care about climate change by making sure any investments you and your university, workplace or pension fund make do not include fossil fuels. Meet with your bank or investment adviser and/or join a divestment campaign at your university.

Fossil fuels are a sunset industry. They're a risk for investors and the planet. As Arnold Schwarzenegger said, "I don't want to be the last investor in Blockbuster as Netflix emerged."

Invest in Renewables

Even if you can't install solar panels or a wind turbine, you can still be a part of the clean-energy economy. Search online for local renewable energy co-ops to join. By becoming a co-op member you will own a slice of its renewable energy projects and can get a return on your investment.

You can also speak to your financial adviser about clean energy/technology investments.

Help Put a Price on Pollution

Putting a price on carbon is one of the most important pillars of any strong climate policy. Carbon pricing sounds boring, but it helps makes polluting activities more expensive and green solutions relatively more affordable, allowing your energy-efficient business and/or household to save money!

Most market economists agree that pricing carbon is an efficient and business-friendly way to reduce emissions. The federal government is working with the provinces and territories to put a national price on carbon, but they need your support.

Vote

All levels of government, from municipal to federal, can have a big effect on our ability to lower emissions, prepare and adapt to climate change and shift to a clean-energy economy.

Make sure you are registered to vote and then get informed for all elections—not just the federal ones that get most of the media attention. Research the party, ask questions about climate change at town halls or debates and let your candidates know you are voting for the climate. Candidates often hold a wide range of positions on climate change, so your vote really matters.

If you are too young to vote, encourage your class or school to join a Student Vote program, a parallel election for students under voting age that provides the opportunity to experience participation in the election process.

Tell Your Story, Listen to Others

A healthy planet and stable climate aren't political issues. It's all about families, communities, energy systems and humanity's future. It's important to get everyone on board, working toward climate solutions.

People are more often influenced by friends than by experts, so make sure to talk about climate change with friends and family. Tell your stories—about changes you've seen where you live, how climate change has affected you, and the changes you're making to lessen your impact. Encourage friends and family to explore the top 10 things they can do about climate change.

Join us on Facebook, Twitter and Instagram to share ideas and articles, write comments and help get the word out. Or, write your own letter to the editor about climate action in your local paper.

Choices Regarding Food Can Help Address Climate Change

Andy Murdock

Andy Murdock is a science and sustainability journalist who attended University of California, Berkeley.

Two important statistics help frame any discussion about food waste: 1.3 metric gigatons of edible food goes to waste every year and at least 795 million people are undernourished worldwide.

These numbers are nearly impossible to envision, but the general takeaway is this: as millions go hungry, we continue to waste perfectly good food on an enormous scale.

The issue goes beyond hunger: Producing the food we waste takes land, water, labor and other valuable resources. To add insult to injury, food waste is a major source of greenhouse gases, mostly in the form of methane, a pollutant at least 25 times more potent than carbon dioxide.

When we talk about climate pollution, we tend to focus on power plants, transportation and industry. If we think about food at all, it's generally cows and their—ahem—"emissions." Wasted food often gets overlooked, but according to an assessment by the UN Food and Agriculture Organization (FAO), 6.7 percent of all global greenhouse gases come from food waste.

How Big Is the Problem of Food Waste?

If 6.7 percent sounds small, here's one way to put it into perspective. Imagine that all the world's food waste came together to form a country. It wouldn't be a very popular country to live in, but it would have an outsize impact on everyone else: the nation of, Food Waste would be the third largest emitter of greenhouse gases, behind China and the US.

"What You Need to Know About Food Waste and Climate Change," by Andy Murdock, The Regents of the University of California, May 9, 2017. Reprinted by permission.

Just how big is the country of Food Waste? According to the FAO, the land devoted to producing wasted food is roughly 5.4 million square miles, which would make it the second largest country in the world behind Russia. That's an area equivalent to Central America, Mexico, plus the lower 48 states and a big part of Canada used for nothing but producing food we don't eat.

Where Is Food Waste Coming From?

While thinking about food waste as a country helps size up a hard-to-conceptualize problem, it's not entirely fair: Every country in the world contributes to food waste, some more than others.

Globally, roughly half of food waste is created before the food leaves the farm, while the other half happens during processing, distribution and consumption. In developing countries, more waste happens on the farm and in distribution, while in developed countries, the pattern flips, with more waste happening at the retail and consumer level. An analysis of food waste in the US by ReFED found that nearly 85 percent of waste occurs in stores, restaurants and homes.

Food waste happens at every stage, from farm to plate, though the mix of culprits varies region by region, from poor access to proper refrigeration or food labels that encourage wasteful behavior. Food waste isn't simply a problem associated with wealth and abundance; Poor infrastructure, inefficient agricultural systems and regional reliance on specific crops also contribute, making food waste a truly global problem.

Regionally speaking, industrialized Asia contributes the most food waste by volume—nearly 30 percent of the global total—and has the largest carbon footprint. South and Southeast Asia fall in second place in terms of total food waste, while North America (including Oceania) is a distant sixth, with roughly 8 percent of the global total.

Which Foods Have the Biggest Footprint?

In general, plant-based foods are far less greenhouse-gas-intensive than meats—that is, if you have a pound of decomposing fruit and a pound of rotting meat, the meat will produce more greenhouse gases. This pattern holds true even when compared per unit of protein.

Overall, because of the scale of their production, grains produce both the most waste and the most greenhouse gas emissions. Relatively little meat is wasted worldwide, but even small amounts of meat waste produce large amounts of greenhouse gases. Even among meats and dairy products, there is quite a bit of variation in levels of impact: Emissions are highest for beef and lamb, but much lower for pork, chicken, eggs and dairy.

What Can We Do About Food Waste?

It's not all bad news when it comes to food waste. Among the causes of climate change, food waste is perhaps the easiest to deal with and the one where everyone can make an impact in their daily lives.

On a personal level, we can save money and reduce our climate impact by planning meals and only buying food we know we are going to eat. Reducing meat intake and buying local produce can also help reduce our carbon footprint. Portion size control is not only helpful for health reasons, it can also reduce waste. Toss uneaten leftovers and other spoiled food into the compost bin or use your city's green waste program, if it's available.

Policymakers in the US are currently working on new guidelines for food labels to help consumers reduce waste.

Personal Decisions Also Impact the Environment

Damian Carrington

Damian Carrington is the environment editor for the Guardian.

The greatest impact individuals can have in fighting climate change is to have one fewer child, according to a new study that identifies the most effective ways people can cut their carbon emissions.

The next best actions are selling your car, avoiding long flights, and eating a vegetarian diet. These reduce emissions many times more than common green activities, such as recycling, using low energy light bulbs or drying washing on a line. However, the high impact actions are rarely mentioned in government advice and school textbooks, researchers found.

Carbon emissions must fall to two tonnes of CO_2 per person by 2050 to avoid severe global warming, but in the US and Australia emissions are currently 16 tonnes per person and in the UK seven tonnes. "That's obviously a really big change and we wanted to show that individuals have an opportunity to be a part of that," said Kimberly Nicholas, at Lund University in Sweden and one of the research team.

The new study, published in Environmental Research Letters, sets out the impact of different actions on a comparable basis. By far the biggest ultimate impact is having one fewer child, which the researchers calculated equated to a reduction of 58 tonnes of CO_2 for each year of a parent's life.

The figure was calculated by totting up the emissions of the child and all their descendants, then dividing this total by the parent's lifespan. Each parent was ascribed 50% of the child's emissions, 25% of their grandchildren's emissions and so on.

"Want to Fight Climate Change? Have Fewer Children," by Damian Carrington, Guardian News and Media Limited, July 12, 2017. Reprinted by permission.

"We recognise these are deeply personal choices. But we can't ignore the climate effect our lifestyle actually has," said Nicholas. "It is our job as scientists to honestly report the data. Like a doctor who sees the patient is in poor health and might not like the message 'smoking is bad for you,' we are forced to confront the fact that current emission levels are really bad for the planet and human society."

"In life, there are many values on which people make decisions and carbon is only one of them," she added. "I don't have children, but it is a choice I am considering and discussing with my fiance. Because we care so much about climate change that will certainly be one factor we consider in the decision, but it won't be the only one."

Overpopulation has been a controversial factor in the climate change debate, with some pointing out that an American is responsible for 40 times the emissions produced by a Bangladeshi and that overconsumption is the crucial issue. The new research comes a day after researchers blamed overpopulation and overconsumption on the "biological annihilation" of wildlife which has started a mass extinction of species on the planet.

Nicholas said that many of the choices had positive effects as well, such as a healthier diet, as meat consumption in developed countries is about five times higher than recommended by health authorities. Cleaner transport also cuts air pollution, and walking and cycling can reduce obesity. "It is not a sacrifice message," she said. "It is trying to find ways to live a good life in a way that leaves a good atmosphere for the planet. I've found it really positive to make many of these changes."

The researchers analysed dozens of sources from Europe, North America and Japan to calculate the carbon savings individuals in richer nations can make. They found getting rid of a car saved 2.4 tonnes a year, avoiding a return transatlantic flight saved 1.6 tonnes and becoming vegetarian saved 0.8 tonnes a year.

These actions saved the same carbon whichever country an individual lived in, but others varied. The savings from switching to an electric car depend on how green electricity generation is, meaning big savings can be made in Australia but the savings in Belgium are six times lower. Switching your home energy supplier to a green energy company also varied, depending on whether the green energy displaces fossil fuel energy or not.

Nicholas said the low-impact actions, such as recycling, were still worth doing: "All of those are good things to do. But they are more of a beginning than an end. They are certainly not sufficient to tackle the scale of the climate challenge that we face."

The researchers found that government advice in the US, Canada, EU and Australia rarely mentioned the high impact actions, with only the EU citing eating less meat and only Australia citing living without a car. None mentioned having one fewer child. In an analysis of school textbooks on Canada only 4% of the recommendations were high impact.

Chris Goodall, an author on low carbon living and energy, said: "The paper usefully reminds us what matters in the fight against global warming. But in some ways it will just reinforce the suspicion of the political right that the threat of climate change is simply a cover for reducing people's freedom to live as they want.

"Population reduction would probably reduce carbon emissions but we have many other tools for getting global warming under control," he said. "Perhaps more importantly, cutting the number of people on the planet will take hundreds of years. Emissions reduction needs to start now."

Small-Scale Efforts Do Not Have the Impact Needed to Address Climate Change

Oliver Milman

Oliver Milman is an environmental reporter with the Guardian.

Individual cities, regions and businesses across the globe are banding together determinedly to confront climate change—but their emissions reductions are relatively small and don't fully compensate for a recalcitrant US under the Trump administration, a new study has found.

A cavalcade of city mayors, regional government representatives and business executives from around the world will convene in San Francisco next month for a major summit touting the role of action beyond national governments to stave off the worst impacts of climate change.

But the greenhouse gas cuts offered up by these entities are relatively modest, according to new research, placing the onus on nations to raise their ambitions even as the US, the world's second largest emitter, looks to exit the landmark Paris climate agreement.

An evaluation of climate change pledges by nearly 6,000 cities, states and regions, representing 7% of the global population, and more than 2,000 companies that have a combined revenue comparable to the size of the US economy, found a total projected reduction of between 1.5bn to 2.2bn tons of greenhouse gases by 2030.

In some places this action will be significant, such as in the US, where shifts to cleaner energy and energy efficiency by cities and states are on track to contribute half of the emissions reductions promised by the country in the Paris agreement.

"Climate Change: Local Efforts Won't Be Enough to Undo Trump's Inaction, Study Says," by Oliver Milman, Guardian News and Media Limited, August 30, 2018. Reprinted by permission.

But globally these emissions cuts fall short of enabling countries to avoid breaching agreed thresholds for dangerous warming that will trigger increased heatwaves, mightier storms, rising seas and displacement of people.

"When we look at the individual pledges [by cities, regions and businesses] the impact isn't that large so we absolutely need national governments to pull through and do a lot of the heavy lifting," said Dr Angel Hsu, the director of Data-Driven Yale, which led the study.

"The actions of cities, companies and states aren't insignificant but they can't do it by themselves. This shows everyone can be doing more. The current reductions are woefully inadequate and hopefully the actions of other entities will give national governments the confidence to be more ambitious."

The analyzed reductions, taken from nine high-emitting countries such as the US, China, India and Brazil, as well as the European Union, overlap with some national efforts that increase the total contribution of emissions cuts.

But this action isn't sufficient to bridge a gap between the Paris agreement's goal to avoid 2C (3.6F) of global warming, with an aspiration of avoiding a 1.5C increase, and the insufficient emissions reductions put forward by the deal's nearly 200 national signatories.

The agenda of the Trump administration risks making this goal even more challenging. Trump has promised to withdraw the US from the Paris agreement and has unveiled a plan to weaken vehicle emissions standards that could result in more than 1bn tons of extra carbon dioxide over the next 15 years. Last week, Trump's Environmental Protection Agency announced a watered-down climate policy for the energy sector that might even result in emissions rising from coal plants.

Even if every Paris commitment is fully implemented, the world is on track to warm by around 3.3C by the end of the century. Pledges by the likes of Berlin, the Coca-Cola company or even an economic powerhouse like California "while welcome, are not sufficient", said John Sterman, the director of the MIT system dynamics group.

"The world is in a desperate race between accelerating climate change and the innovation needed to cut emissions before it's too late," said Sterman. "Cities, states, and business are in the lead, but they face stiff headwinds from weak national policies and the continued efforts of fossil fuel interests to undermine the innovation we need."

Global greenhouse gas emissions rose slightly last year, after a short period of stasis, highlighting the looming scenario whereby as-yet unproven technology will need to be deployed at a mass scale to suck CO_2 directly from the air or capture and bury it after burning vegetation, known as biomass, for energy.

"We are already in an overshoot situation and it's likely we are already going to have to need to remove carbon from the air," said Klaus Lackner, the director of center for negative carbon emissions at Arizona State University. "The idea we just tighten our belt a bit isn't going to solve the problem. We need to stop using the atmosphere as a dumping ground, abandon fossil fuels, find other sources of energy and deal with the carbon debt we already have.

"Cities getting involved is good and important but we haven't really acknowledged how big and serious the challenge is. We are whistling in the dark."

The Focus of Environmentalism Should Be on Industrial Activity

Eliza Barclay and Umair Irfan

Eliza Barclay is the science and health editor at Vox.com. *Umair Irfan reports on climate change, energy, and the environment for* Vox.

Climate scientists told us late last year in the National Climate Assessment that the United States is already experiencing severe and costly impacts of a changing climate. In a separate United Nations report released in October, scientists reported that limiting global warming to 1.5 degrees Celsius would require a gargantuan global effort—and that we have roughly 12 years to do it. But how?

One bright spot to remember this Earth Day is that we already have the tools we need.

Let's make something clear, though: The emissions we need to focus on now are the ones at the industrial, corporate level.

According to the Carbon Majors Database, 71 percent of global greenhouse gas emissions since 1988 can be traced back to just 100 fossil fuel companies. Hitting the 1.5°C or 2°C goals means these corporations, their customers, and other large enterprises must phase out fossil fuels (more aggressively than what Shell laid out in its vision for a zero-carbon world).

Governments will also have to come up with tax schemes to generate new revenue for investment in and incentives for renewable energy, reforestation, and carbon removal technologies. And we need to vote for leaders who will deliver on them.

The Trump administration is obviously contributing little to these efforts, trying its best to roll back Obama's suite of climate policies and enable the continuation of fossil fuel dominance. But a growing number of younger leaders around the world understand

"10 Ways to Accelerate Progress Against Climate Change," by Eliza Barclay and Umair Irfan, Vox Media, Inc., November 26, 2018. Reprinted by permission.

what's at stake and are pushing for more ambitious goals, like the ones outlined in the Green New Deal.

Here are some examples of strategies that are working and need to be rolled out worldwide:

Price Carbon Emissions

By adding a cost to emitting greenhouse gases, you create an incentive to produce less of them and switch to alternatives.

It's hard to convince someone to pay for something if they can get it for free. Right now, much of the world can dump their greenhouse gases in the atmosphere at no charge. And we don't have many straightforward ways to value the carbon that trees and algae help pull out of the atmosphere.

Though the new Intergovernmental Panel on Climate Change (IPCC) report didn't explicitly discuss the economics of fighting climate change, the authors highlighted at a press conference that attaching a price tag to greenhouse gases is a critical step in limiting warming. "Carbon pricing and the right economic signals are going to be part of the mix," said Jim Skea, co-chair of IPCC Working Group III.

Even fossil fuel giant ExxonMobil is campaigning for a carbon tax.

To date, at least 40 countries have priced carbon in some form. Some have done it through a carbon tax. Cap-and-trade schemes for carbon dioxide are also underway, like the European Union's Emissions Trading System. China now runs the world's largest carbon trading market. Even some regions in the United States have cap-and-trade schemes, like the Regional Greenhouse Gas Initiative among eastern states.

But, as our colleague David Roberts wrote on Twitter, "A price on carbon of some sort is, wonks almost universally agree, an important part of a comprehensive climate strategy. But the details make all the difference in whether it's regressive or not, effective or not, popular or not, passable or not."

Subsidize Clean Energy and End Subsidies for Dirty Energy

Renewable energy sources like wind and solar power have already become dramatically more affordable. In the United States, renewables are cost-competitive with fossil fuels in some markets. In Europe, new unsubsidized renewable energy projects are coming online.

From a market standpoint, it might seem like the time is near for pulling the plug on subsidies to renewables. But if your goal is to fight climate change, it makes more sense to keep giving cleaner energy sources a boost.

The fossil fuel industry is meanwhile still getting a number of direct and indirect subsidies. In the US, these subsidies can amount to $20 billion a year. Globally, it's about $260 billion per year. Getting rid of government support for these fuels seems like a no-brainer. But yes, the massive political influence of fossil fuels means this will continue to be extremely hard.

Close Coals Plants, and Cut Off the Fossil Fuel Supply in Other Ways

The world is still opening tens of thousands of megawatts of coal-fired power capacity every year.

Each of these plants represents decades of further greenhouse gas emissions. Although the rate of new coal power plants is declining, that's not enough. We still need to shut down the oldest, dirtiest coal power plants and prevent new ones from coming online.

According to the IPCC, to stay on track for climate goals, global coal consumption would have to decline by two-thirds by 2030.

And while natural gas emits about half the greenhouse gases of coal, the quantity isn't zero, so these generators are in the cross-hairs too.

Some countries are already taking steps to shut off fossil fuel power. German Chancellor Angela Merkel has assembled a panel to figure out when the country can close all of its coal plants. The

United Kingdom, meanwhile, has pledged to end its coal use by 2025.

Economists have also argued that countries should use supply-side tactics to restrict the supply of fossil fuels in other ways, too: like opting against new oil and gas pipelines, refineries, and export terminals.

Electrify Everything and Get More Efficient

Energy efficiency is the lowest of the low-hanging fruit in fighting climate change.

Increasing fuel economy, insulating buildings, and upgrading lighting are all small incremental changes that add up to dramatic reductions in energy use, curbing greenhouse gas emissions.

It's also often the cheapest tactic.

"The combined evidence suggests that aggressive policies addressing energy efficiency are central in keeping 1.5°C within reach and lowering energy system and mitigation costs," according to the new IPCC report.

Buildings, for example, account for roughly one-third of global energy use and about a quarter of total greenhouse gas emissions. To stay on track for 1.5°C of warming, indoor heating and cooling demands would have to decline by at least one-third by 2050.

Many countries already have building codes that require new structures to use state-of-the-art HVAC systems, double-pane glass windows, and energy-saving appliances. But most of the buildings that are standing now will still exist in 2050, so retrofitting existing homes and offices to use less energy needs to be a major policy priority.

Another way to use our resources more efficiently is to electrify everything: oil heaters, diesel trucks, gas stoves. That way, as our sources of electricity get cleaner, they pay climate dividends throughout the rest of the electrified economy. And products like electric cars are far more energy-efficient than their gasoline-powered counterparts.

However, we need financing, incentives, and penalties to push the global economy to do more with less.

Invest in Innovation

Perhaps the best tools to fight climate change haven't been invented yet—a battery that can store gobs of energy for months, a solar panel that's twice as efficient, a crop that makes biofuels cheaper than petroleum, or something even better, beyond our imaginations.

So while we clamp down on heavy emitters and deploy cleaner alternatives, we also need to come up with new answers to climate change.

That means investing in basic research and development. It also means helping nascent technologies get out of the laboratory and onto the power grid, whether through loans, grants, or regulations.

The United States already has a framework for this. The Department of Energy runs the Advanced Research Projects Agency-Energy (ARPA-E), a small federal program that funds high-risk, high-reward energy projects with an eye toward fighting climate change. It's backed projects ranging from flow batteries to wide bandgap semiconductors.

While analysts have argued that programs like ARPA-E increase America's competitiveness and that the world needs more innovation initiatives for clean energy, the Trump administration has repeatedly tried to zero out its $353 million budget. Congress has nonetheless kept it in place and gave the program a boost in the last spending bill.

End Production and Sales of Cars, Trucks, and Buses that Run on Fossil Fuels

Within a few decades, we are likely to see a worldwide transition away from vehicles that run on gas toward ones that use electricity.

But there's a lot of uncertainty about how quickly it will happen. And governments have to hurry it along by phasing out the production and sale of gas and diesel vehicles altogether and helping consumers purchase EVs instead.

Fortunately, there's a lot of momentum building. In 2017, both China and India, along with a few European countries, announced plans to end sales of gas and diesel vehicles. China is hustling toward that goal by providing incentives to manufacturers of electric car and bus makers, as well as subsidies to consumers who purchase EVs to the tune of $10,000 per vehicle on average.

The US is lagging, as per usual, despite the fact our transportation sector today emits more carbon than any other sector of the economy. California, however, is going full speed ahead on EV policy. Its target is 5 million zero-emissions vehicles by 2030 and 250,000 zero-emission vehicle chargers—including 10,000 DC fast chargers—by 2025.

Require "Zero Deforestation" Supply Chains

Tropical forests in Latin America, Southeast Asia, and Central Africa are essential for keeping carbon in the ground and maintaining the climate.

And the current rate that we're clearing them—to make way for cattle ranches, as well as palm oil, soy, and wood products—is putting us on a course for rapid climate change, with intensifying cycles of extreme droughts, more heat, and more forest fires.

All told, deforestation accounts for an estimated 15 percent of total greenhouse gas emissions.

Halting deforestation can't be done from afar; it requires working closely with local communities who live in and rely on forests. But governments and corporations can also be pressured to buy commodities only from forest regions certified as "deforestation-free."

Norway, for instance, now has a "zero deforestation policy," where it has committed to ensuring "that public procurements do not contribute to deforestation of the rainforest." Hundreds of companies have made zero-deforestation commitments, too, but we still have a long way to go before they're airtight and working.

If we could stop deforestation, restore some of the forests we've cut down, and improve forestry practices, we could remove 7 billion metric tons of carbon from the atmosphere annually—equal to eliminating 1.5 billion cars, according to the Climate and Land Use Alliance.

Keep Aging Nuclear Plants Running

Nuclear power currently is responsible for about 20 percent of US electricity—and 50 percent of its carbon-free electricity. As Vox's David Roberts has noted, the US could lose a lot of this power if some 15 to 20 nuclear plants at risk of closing shut down in the next five to 10 years. Which means that, "saving it, or at least as much of it as possible, seems like an obvious and urgent priority for anyone who values decarbonization."

Fortunately, Dave also looked at how we could keep these plants open. Near the top of the list is a relatively modest national carbon price.

But since we can't count on a carbon price in the immediate future, it's worth looking at the other state-level hacks—like zero emissions credits, paid for by a small tariff on power bills—already being deployed to keep nuclear plants running.

Other countries are also wrestling with the future of their nuclear plants. Germany committed to shutting down all of its nuclear reactors by 2022, but the country is now likely to miss its emissions reduction targets. France is now weighing whether to extend the operating life of some of its aging nuclear power plants.

Discourage Meat and Dairy Consumption, Encourage Plant-Based Diets

Producing animal products, particularly beef and dairy, creates the majority of food-related greenhouse emissions, while the food supply chain overall creates 26 percent of total emissions. The most obvious way to bring these emissions down would be to engineer a massive shift in dietary patterns, reducing our meat and dairy consumption and shrinking the livestock sector.

"GHG emissions cannot be sufficiently mitigated without dietary changes towards more plant-based diets," as Marco Springmann of the Oxford Martin Program on the Future of Food and co-authors wrote in a paper published Wednesday in the journal *Nature*.

But again, this is not so much about individual choices. This is about asking our leaders, institutions, and employers to make dietary change a priority to truly shift markets and lower emissions. Trouble is, no country has had significant success yet with reducing its meat consumption. And as Springmann and his co-authors note, "providing information without additional economic or environmental changes has a limited influence on behavior."

The kinds of changes we need, they write, include "media and education campaigns; labeling and consumer information; fiscal measures, such as taxation, subsidies, and other economic incentives; school and workplace approaches; local environmental changes; and direct restriction and mandates."

It's that last one, "direct restriction and mandates," that's most interesting, most daring, and most essential to try immediately.

Some countries like China are beginning to work meat consumption reduction goals into their dietary guidelines. The US should do that too in its next update in 2020. There's also the Cool Food Pledge, a platform launched in September by the World Resources Institute, to help food service providers slash food-related emissions by 25 percent by 2030. So far, a few companies and institutions have signed up, including Morgan Stanley, UC Davis Medical Center, and Genentech.

Companies and governments could also follow WeWork's lead and stop serving or paying for meat at company events.

We need many more experiments like this. We still have no idea how to go about dietary change on the scale that's necessary to reduce livestock-related emissions.

Remove Carbon Dioxide from the Atmosphere

Every scenario outlined by the IPCC report counts on pulling carbon dioxide out of the air. However, many of technologies needed to do this are in their infancy.

Carbon dioxide removal (CDR) tactics range from the straightforward (like planting forests) to the novel (like scrubbing carbon dioxide straight from the air).

Governments will need to invest more in CDR technology to improve its effectiveness and bring down costs. Policies like renewable portfolio standards, feed-in tariffs, and investment tax credits can help drive the deployment of CDR, as Julio Friedmann, a researcher at Columbia University who studies carbon capture, noted recently in The Hill. But the biggest thing CDR companies need to blossom is a price on carbon.

Organizations to Contact

The editors have compiled the following list of organizations concerned with the issues debated in this book. The descriptions are derived from materials provided by the organizations. All have publications or information available for interested readers. This list was compiled on the date of publication of the present volume; the information provided here may change. Be aware that many organizations take several weeks or longer to respond to inquiries, so allow as much time as possible.

Environmental Defense Fund (EDF)
257 Park Avenue South
New York, NY 10010
phone: (212) 505-2100
email: www.edf.org/contact
website: www.edf.org

The EDF is a scientist-founded organization that considers economic solutions to climate-related issues, including food security. The group advocates for policies that safeguard the planet and partners with organizations, governments, and businesses to implement plans. Its focus is international.

Environmental Protection Agency (EPA)
1200 Pennsylvania Avenue NW
Washington, DC 20460
phone: (202) 564-4700
website: www.epa.gov

The EPA is the federal agency responsible for safeguarding the environment in the United States. To do so, the EPA implements and suggests regulations on industries harmful to the environment, publishes reports on environmental issues, and maintains studies of environmental topics.

European Environment Agency (EEA)
Kongens Nytorv 6
1050 Copenhagen K
Denmark
phone: +45 3336 7100
website: www.eea.europa.eu

The EEA is a European Union agency charged with analyzing climate data and science in order to understand climate change. The agency publishes reports and studies on environmental issues, as well as policy suggestions. It is focused on the European Union.

Foundation for Environmental Education (FEE)
Scandiagade 13
2450 Copenhagen SV
Denmark
phone: +45 7022 2427
email: info@fee.global
website: www.fee.global

The FEE is an international organization that works to educate the public on issues of environmentalism. The group works with seventy-seven countries to run programs and campaigns for awareness regarding environmentalism.

Global Green Growth Institute (GGGI)
19F Jeongdong Building
21-15 Jeongdong-gil
Jung-gu, Seoul 04518
Republic of Korea
phone: +82 70 7117 9982
email: gggi.org/contact
website: www.gggi.org

The GGGI is the governing body of an international treaty organization that supports environmentally friendly development in emerging economies. It works with small and developing economic states to ensure climate-friendly policies are put in place.

Intergovernmental Panel on Climate Change (IPCC)
7biz, avenue de la Paix
Case postale 2300
CH-1211 Geneva 2
Switzerland
phone: +41 0 22 730 81 11
email: wmo@wmo.int
website: www.ipcc.ch

The IPCC is an intergovermental body of the UN that was established under the World Meteorological Organization. It is responsible for the analysis and study of climate data and publishes authoritative reports on climate change.

Natural Resources Defense Council (NRDC)
40 West 20th Street, 11th Floor
New York, NY 10011
phone: (212) 727-2700
email: nrdcinfo@nrdc.org
website: www.nrdc.org

The NRDC uses advocacy, business partnerships, litigation, and other means to ensure the conservation of natural resources and spaces. It works on topics related to climate change, endangered species, food security, and clean water among other topics.

Sierra Club
2102 Webster Street, Suite 1300
Oakland, CA 94612
phone: (415) 977-5500
email: information@sierraclub.org
website: www.sierraclub.org

The Sierra Club is a large membership organization that advocates for environmental issues. It works on topics related to conservation, climate change, pollution, and similar issues.

Trust for Public Land (TPL)
100 M Street SE, Suite 700
Washington, DC 20003
phone: (202) 543-7552
email: washdc@tpl.org
website: www.tpl.org

The TPL works to protect public lands and to encourage people to engage with these spaces. The organization also works with cities to create smart, climate-friendly policies and partners with parks and cities to expand or enhance natural spaces.

UN Environment Programme
United Nations Avenue, Gigiri
PO Box 30552
00100 Nairobi
Kenya
phone: +254 020 762 1234
email: unenvironment-info@un.org
website: www.unenvironment.org

The UN Environment Programme is the United Nation's agency responsible for setting and implementing environmental policy on a global level. It works with experts from around the world to establish best practices, publish reports on initiatives, and explore possible solutions to issues impacting the environment. It is international in scope.

Bibliography

Books

Donald Anderson, *Below Freezing: Elegy for the Melting Planet.* Santa Fe, NM: University of New Mexico Press, 2018.

Michael Berners-Lee, *There Is No Planet B.* Cambridge, UK: Cambridge University Press, 2019.

Michael Bloomberg and Carl Pope, *Climate of Hope: How Cities, Businesses, and Citizens Can Save the Planet.* New York, NY: St Martin's Press, 2017.

Douglas Farr, *Sustainable Nation: Urban Design Patterns for the Future.* New York, NY: Wiley, 2018.

L. S. Gardiner, *Tales from an Uncertain World.* Iowa City, IA; University of Iowa Press, 2018.

Naomi Klein, *This Changes Everything: Capitalism vs. The Climate.* New York, NY: Simon & Schuster, 2014.

Elizabeth Kolbert, *The Sixth Extinction: An Unnatural History.* New York, NY: Henry Holt & Co, 2014.

Linda Marsa, *Fevered: How a Hotter Planet Will Hurt Our Health and How We Can Save Ourselves.* New York, NY: Rodale, 2013.

Jeff Nesbit, *This Is the Way the World Ends.* New York, NY: Thomas Dunne Books, 2018.

Hannah Nordhaus, *The Beekeeper's Lament: How One Man and Half a Billion Honey Bees Help Feed America.* New York, NY: Harper Perennial, 2011.

Lisa Palmer, *Hot, Hungry Planet: The Fight to Stop a Global Food Crisis in the Face of Climate Change.* New York, NY: St. Martin's Press, 2017.

Mary Robinson, *Climate Justice*. New York, NY: Bloomsbury, 2018.

Elizabeth Rush, *Rising: Dispatches from the New American Shore*. New York, NY: Milkweed Editions, 2018.

Mark C. Serreze, *Brave New Arctic*. Princeton, NJ: Princeton University Press, 2018.

William T. Vollmann, *No Immediate Danger*. New York, NY: Penguin Books, 2019.

Periodicals and Internet Sources

S. Elizabeth Birnbaum and Jacqueline Savitz, "The Deepwater Horizon Threat," *New York Times*, April 16, 2014. https://www.nytimes.com/2014/04/17/opinion/the-deepwater-horizon-threat.html.

"Effects of Climate Change 'Irreversible,' U.N. Panel Warns in Report," Consortium for Ocean Leadership, November 13, 2014. https://oceanleadership.org/effects-climate-change-irreversible-u-n-panel-warns-report/.

"Global Warming of 1.5 degrees C," Intergovernmental Panel on Climate Change, October 8, 2018. https://www.ipcc.ch/sr15/.

Robert Jay Lifton, "Our Changing Climate Mindset," *New York Times*. October 7, 2017. https://www.nytimes.com/2017/10/07/opinion/sunday/hurricanes-climate-public-opinion.html.

Rick Noack, "Ireland and Britain Declare Climate Emergencies. Will It Make A Difference?" *Washington Post*, May 10, 2019. https://www.washingtonpost.com/world/2019/05/10/ireland-britain-declare-climate-emergencies-will-it-make-difference/?utm_term=.e3cd85893638.

Jo-Ellen Parry and Anika Terton, "How Are Vulnerable Countries Adapting to Climate Change?" International

Institute for Sustainable Development. https://www.iisd.org/faq/adapting-to-climate-change/.

Andrew Revkin, "Climate Change First Became News 30 Years Ago. Why Haven't We Fixed It?" *National Geographic*, July 2018. https://www.nationalgeographic.com/magazine/2018/07/embark-essay-climate-change-pollution-revkin/.

Roddy Scheer and Doug Moss, "Is It Too Late to Avoid the Worst Impacts of Climate Change?" *Scientific American*. https://www.scientificamerican.com/article/reducing-atmospheric-co2/?redirect=1.

Donald Wuebbles, David W. Fahey, and Kathy A. Hibbard, "How Will Climate Change Affect the United States in Decades to Come?" American Geophysical Union, November 3, 2017. https://eos.org/features/how-will-climate-change-affect-the-united-states-in-decades-to-come.

Robin Young and Jack Mitchell, "Humans Have 30 Years to Stave Off Climate Catastrophe, 'Uninhabitable Earth' Author Says," WBUR, May 13, 2019. https://www.wbur.org/hereandnow/2019/05/13/climate-change-uninhabitable-earth-david-wallace-wells.

Index

O

Obama, Barack, 36, 157

P

Paris Agreement, 32, 33, 34, 40,
41, 42, 47–48, 96, 154, 155
Planete Energies, 32–35
polar regions, 62–63
private sector, 36–39, 40–41

R

renewable energy, 26, 27, 31,
36, 38–39, 92–93, 143,
145, 159
Rio Earth Summit, 32–33, 34
Rio+20 Conference, 34–35
Ritter, Bill, Jr., 36–39
Russia, 30, 35

S

sea levels, rising, 14, 58, 59,
60, 61, 63, 107, 133, 143
shelter, effects on, 57
solar power, 28–29, 31, 37,
92–93
South America, 61
Sterman, John, 156

T

technology to fight climate
change, 91–95, 134–138
transportation emissions,
reduction of, 143–144

U

Union of Concerned
Scientists, 73–77, 107–111
United Kingdom, 35, 41
United Nations, 16, 22, 40–41,
64, 91, 96
Environmental
Programme, 21, 41
Food and Agricultural
Organization (FAO),
78–90, 148
Framework Convention on
Climate Change, 33, 34,
44, 45, 47–48
United States
emissions, 31, 35, 45, 50, 154
Kyoto Protocol and, 33
promotion of clean energy
technologies, 36–37
Trump administration
reversal of clean power
plans, 36, 37, 38, 41, 154,
155, 157, 161

W

water supply and quality,
54–55, 58–59, 60, 61, 63,
66, 109–110, 131
Watson, James E. M., 43–48
weather, severe, 14, 23–24,
41, 57, 68, 73–77, 80, 81,
108–109, 143
wind power, 31, 37, 93